TERRITORIAL DEVELOPMENT

IRELAND

LOCAL PARTNERSHIPS AND SOCIAL INNOVATION

Prepared by Professor Charles Sabel
and the LEED Programme

GU00801609

ORGANISATION FOR ECONOMIC CO-OPERATION AND DEVELOPMENT

ORGANISATION FOR ECONOMIC CO-OPERATION AND DEVELOPMENT

Pursuant to Article 1 of the Convention signed in Paris on 14th December 1960, and which came into force on 30th September 1961, the Organisation for Economic Co-operation and Development (OECD) shall promote policies designed:

- to achieve the highest sustainable economic growth and employment and a rising standard of living in Member countries, while maintaining financial stability, and thus to contribute to the development of the world economy;
- to contribute to sound economic expansion in Member as well as non-member countries in the process of economic development; and
- to contribute to the expansion of world trade on a multilateral, non-discriminatory basis in accordance with international obligations.

The original Member countries of the OECD are Austria, Belgium, Canada, Denmark, France, Germany, Greece, Iceland, Ireland, Italy, Luxembourg, the Netherlands, Norway, Portugal, Spain, Sweden, Switzerland, Turkey, the United Kingdom and the United States. The following countries became Members subsequently through accession at the dates indicated hereafter: Japan (28th April 1964), Finland (28th January 1969), Australia (7th June 1971), New Zealand (29th May 1973), Mexico (18th May 1994) and the Czech Republic (21st December 1995). The Commission of the European Communities takes part in the work of the OECD (Article 13 of the OECD Convention).

Publié en français sous le titre :

IRLANDE
PARTENARIATS LOCAUX ET INNOVATION SOCIALE

FOREWORD

In an increasingly complex and interdependent world, many of the issues governments have to address – ranging from improving economic competitiveness to fighting unemployment and combating social exclusion – have an important spatial element. Because national macroeconomic and structural policies alone are unable to manage this diversity, policies addressing specific issues in target areas are needed to complement and reinforce the traditional range of policy instruments. As well as improving the efficiency of public policymaking, area-based approaches also permit policies to be more socially inclusive and help ensure the social stability and cohesion without which economic growth and structural adjustment will be obstructed. In recognition of this, the OECD Council created the Territorial Development Service, which brings together units dealing with local, regional, rural and urban policy issues. Thus, the initiatives of the Irish government reviewed in this report are consistent with, and even exemplify, trends in policy analysis within the OECD.

It is in this context that the Local Economic and Employment Development (LEED) Programme of the OECD was invited by the Irish Government to undertake this study. Mr. Gay Mitchell, T.D., Minister for European Affairs and Local Development, along with officials of the Department of Enterprise and Employment and the Department of the Taoiseach, felt that it was important to have the benefit of objective international expertise in order to help realise the full potential of the local development initiatives that have been established in the past few years. Minister Mitchell's wish was that this report could make a significant contribution to the process of self-evaluation and further development of policy in the field of local development, not only in Ireland but also elsewhere in the OECD.

Over the past few years, the Irish Government has introduced a series of institutional innovations aimed particularly at reducing the incidence and mitigating the effects of long-term unemployment. The core of the experiment was the creation of urban and rural area-based partnerships to address issues of social exclusion in a more flexible, decentralised and participative way. These partnerships exert a strong influence over an increasing part of the local activities and expenditures of the agencies of national government (including training, welfare and enterprise promotion) and can tailor their activities according to local circumstances and insist on the provision of services perceived as necessary by the partnership.

This report presents compelling evidence of the potential of this local partnership approach as the springboard to a new response to economic and social problems. The Irish local development groups discussed here, notably the Area-Based Partnerships but also other similar entities, embody a number of features in terms of their organisation and structure that are extremely innovative and could well serve as a model for similar initiatives elsewhere. Moreover, as this report shows, they have produced results which suggest that some of the most pressing issues affecting OECD countries can be tackled in a manner that is effective, innovative and oriented towards broader principles such as social justice and subsidiarity.

Several particular elements that distinguish the local partnership response are highlighted in the report:

- the partnerships have provided models for widening participation in processes of change within the economy and society. The partnerships act as conduits for local involvement in formulating strategies, channelling resources and implementing policies to deal with issues of local, but also national and international, concern, such as unemployment and inequality;

- policies undertaken through the partnerships draw directly on local experiences; for example, programmes for the unemployed are set up by local unemployed people themselves and enterprise creation programmes build on the expertise of local businessmen;

- local partnerships have succeeded in adapting the objectives and resource allocation of state agencies within their areas in order to better meet local needs;

- the national policies of social welfare provision have been directly affected by the activities of local development groups who have communicated their concerns about problems of targeting and emphasis to the central government; and

- local partnerships have given a positive, practical example of hitherto somewhat abstract concepts such as public-private partnership, area-based programming and even subsidiarity.

This report describes specific partnership groups in order to analyse their method of operation and shows how the attention paid at the outset to giving local interests a real voice has borne fruit in a stream of innovative projects which are now influencing and informing the activities of government. Although not all partnership groups are examined in this report, the examples presented are sufficient to suggest that if all local development activities can be helped to match the achievements of the best, then the approach has enormous potential for Ireland and for all OECD countries.

Despite these initial successes, the anomalous character of the partnership programme within the public administration represents a weakness that needs to be addressed. This weakness revolves around three main issues: institutional legitimacy, democratic legitimacy and calls for rationalisation, which together or separately could threaten the continued existence of the partnership groups in their present form. The recommendations of this report therefore deal with how to strengthen the institutional place of local development groups, help them respond to questions of accountability and attempt to define their role *vis-à-vis* that of other local development groups. Fundamentally, we conclude that a more stable framework needs to be put in place, but that the partnerships must retain the freedom to innovate that defines the programmes in their present form. Given a more stable footing, through a process we term "democratic experimentalism", the local partnerships could have an important role to play in provoking reform of the public administration on the basis of active participation by citizens in the decisions that shape their lives.

The OECD invited Dr. Charles Sabel of the Columbia Law School to lead this study. He, assisted by the OECD Secretariat, is the author of this report. It follows an expert study group that visited Ireland in October 1995. The group was led by Charles Sabel and comprised Jean-Claude Bontron, Director, SEGESA, France, John Elliott, Head of the Training and Enterprise Council (TEC) Research and Evaluation Department, UK, Michael Förschner, Ministry of Labour and Social Affairs, Austria, Hans Pflaumer, former State Secretary for Regional Policy, Germany, Paavo Saikkonen, Ministry of Labour, Finland, and Nilgun Tas, Vice-President, Small and Medium Industry Development Organisation, Turkey. Parts of Chapter 2 are based on the conclusions of an *ad hoc* contact group assembled by Rory O'Donnell, National Economic and Social Council, Dublin, and David Jacobson, Dublin City University. The views expressed by the authors do not necessarily reflect those of individual study group members. It is published on the responsibility of the Secretary-General of the OECD.

The OECD would particularly like to thank Mr. Richard Bruton, Minister for Enterprise and Employment, Secretary Kevin Bonner and Mr. Paul Cullen of the Department of Enterprise and Employment, Minister of State Gay Mitchell and Mr. Dermot McCarthy of the Department of the Taoiseach, and Mr. Rory O'Donnell of the National Economic and Social Council for their assistance with the preparation of the report, and, of course, all of the people who welcomed the study group on their visit to Ireland.

TABLE OF CONTENTS

Chapter 4
Projects and Partnerships: Transforming the Local Context

Chapter 5
Conclusions

INTRODUCTION AND STRUCTURE OF THE REPORT

INTRODUCTION

Ireland is engaged in an innovative experiment to reduce the incidence and mitigate the effects of unemployment while further encouraging the development of an open, competitive economy. At the core of that experiment are 38 Area-Based Partnerships (initially 12) in urban and rural communities created by the Irish Government and the Structural Fund of the European Union (EU) beginning in 1991. The task and opportunity of these partnerships is to reconsider the problems of un- and under-employment within their home jurisdictions and devise effective responses to them that the central government alone could not discover, but to which it may refer in reforming its own administrative structures and, above all, in improving the connection between these structures and local communities.

Legally, the partnerships are independent corporations under Irish company law. Their boards bring together representatives of local community interests including the unemployed, representatives of the national social partner organisations of labour and business, and local or regional representatives of the national social welfare, training, or economic development administrations. Through this structure, the partnerships often have *de facto* authority over a significant share of the local activities and expenditures of core agencies of the national government. In addition, they have the right to provide services and build institutions not contemplated by the statutory bodies. They thus simultaneously pursue area-based economic development and the local, integrated implementation of national programmes connected to it; and they do so in a way that blurs familiar distinctions between public and private, national and local, and representative and participative democracy.

The preliminary results of this effort to foster development and welfare through new forms of public and private local co-ordination are quite promising, if still inconclusive. In five years of operation, urban partnerships have developed innovative techniques for retraining and placing the long-term unemployed and for building potentially self-sustaining firms that provide both training and jobs for those out of work. They have also established new programmes to help early school leavers and single mothers, and to encourage community policing and the management of housing estates by their tenants. Rural partnerships have found ways to increase employment opportunities for under- rather than unemployed groups and to rebuild communities depleted by out-migration.

Together these innovations may form the foundation of a new model for transferring marketable skills to vulnerable groups and communities, unexpectedly providing the opportunity for them to participate in the kinds of activity characteristic of the modern sector of the economy from which they are normally excluded. These innovations, moreover, are accompanied by local proposals for adjustments to the rules governing eligibility for social welfare benefits. These adjusments make participation in the new programmes broadly affordable and attractive, and remove the disincentives that often deter the most needy from exploring their possibilities. All of this activity grows out of and reinforces the need for an exchange of views and proposals between public and para-public agencies and the persons who use their services that is subtly reshaping their shared understanding of which local problems to address and how. One result of this mutual dedication to an urgent, common task is remarkable care in the use of resources and, so far, avoidance of the self-interest that might jeopardise the reform project.

But these promising beginnings are little more than that, and many of the harshest tests of the partnerships and their innovations surely lie ahead. The threats to their continued vitality and expansion are many. First, there is the vulnerability that results from the partnerships' anomalous character. The discretion they exercise in the control of public resources is nowhere authorised by precise administrative rules nor sanctioned directly by the vote of concerned citizens, or even indirectly through a mandate from their local elected representatives. These anomalies invite criticism from civil servants or elected public officials because they view the partnerships as a challenge to their authority, or, less narrowly, because the uncontrolled delegation of authority to groups of uncertain legitimacy offends their sense of democratic propriety, legal order or public accountability. This criticism is in part blunted by the fact that at least half of the partnerships' current funding originates in Brussels. But if the origins of the partnerships' funds make them less perturbing as a claimant on domestic resources, those same origins redouble the suspicion in some quarters that the partnerships are an artificial and extraneous body. Second, there are the vulnerabilities associated with the confusing profusion of new, self-avowedly innovative institutions, some with overlapping jurisdictions.

The partnerships are at the core of a new localism in Ireland, but they are not alone. They were preceded and in part inspired in Ireland by other local development partnership initiatives, particularly in rural areas; they have in turn spurred development by the government of County Strategy Groups to help co-ordinate the projects that it has launched. The very novelty of these institutions makes it impossible to specify exactly the division of labour between them, to say nothing of whether each is well-suited to its task. As conflicts and insufficiencies have begun to emerge, so too, we will see, have calls for simplification that, at the limit, would put the new entities under the supervision of the old.

Third, it is unclear what lessons, if any, the central offices of the national welfare and development agencies, on the one hand, and the social partner associations, on the other, are drawing from the new forms of collaboration between their local representatives and the successful partnerships. Nor, for that matter, is it even clear that partnerships in similar circumstances are learning from one another's successes and failures. But if successes are not generalised through some combination of national reform and local adaptation, it will be impossible to test whether, taken together and extended, the innovations can make a large enough improvement to the well-being of communities to justify the substantial engagement of volunteers on which their progress until now has depended. If local business groups and community associations despair of progress, their representatives will stop volunteering, the local consensus that animates the partnerships will weaken and co-operation will turn to opportunism.

Finally, all these vulnerabilities are exacerbated by the imponderables associated with the continuation of financial support from the EU. The current arrangement, negotiated between the Irish Government and the European Commission, ends in 1999. By then, the Irish economy, for reasons to be discussed below, may no longer qualify for assistance on anything approaching the current scale. If the problems of legitimacy, confusions of jurisdiction, and erratic exchanges among the partnerships themselves and between them and the central authorities are not being successfully addressed before the scheduled renegotiation of financing, there is little chance of resuming the process afterwards.

But despite its uncertain outcome, the Irish situation demands broad attention now. The problems to which the experiments respond are common, almost universal among OECD countries. The responses they have begun to articulate, while distinct to Ireland, seem in principle widely applicable. The division of Irish society into a substantial majority that prospers from the spread of the new, highly flexible economy and a minority that subsists, un- or under-employed, with public assistance at the margins of this prosperity is one that, in one form or another, besets almost all advanced countries. The failure of centrally conceived and administered programmes of welfare, training, and job creation to mitigate this division is, again, the rule in the advanced countries, not an Irish exception. Even the effort to correct the shortcomings of such programmes or find alternatives to them through decentralisation of decision making is commonplace in the advanced countries. But beyond these commonalities, the Irish experience is distinct in its most general ambitions, in the institutional and economic setting in which those ambitions are pursued, and, as a result, in its initial discoveries.

Take first the difference of intent. In many countries, decentralisation amounts to a loss of confidence not only in the national programmes of social welfare, but in the reformability of central or even local government, and especially in the capacity of any public programme to effectively help the marginalised or those at risk of becoming so. For this reason, such decentralisation has often been accompanied by rigorous efforts to decrease the availability and attractiveness of welfare benefits and correspondingly increase the appeal of regular employment. The expectation is that the self-discipline taught by continuous work will help compensate for the lack of morale induced by dependence on welfare.

In Ireland, by contrast, decentralisation started with a sustained effort, beginning in the late-1980s, to establish the type of concerted action by the social partners at the national level that assures the macroeconomic stability propitious to growth in an open economy, while securing the well-being of the most vulnerable. The Irish attempt at concerted action thus began just when undertakings with similar goals were being abandoned in other countries as unwieldy and capriciously selective in the distribution of benefits. Acknowledgement of these shortcomings suggested, among other things, the formation in Ireland of the local partnerships as a means of extending the advantages of reform and adjustment to groups that might not otherwise benefit immediately from an improvement in the national economy. The partnerships may be taken, therefore, as an expression of the hope that those most in need can benefit from and contribute to a society's efforts to increase its adaptive capacity by reshaping its public self.

These experiments in inclusion were launched under unusually flexible institutional and economic conditions. Throughout the 1980s, Ireland had, by any measure, a centralised system both of social welfare provision and of disbursing funds for economic development. As a result of this centralisation, local government atrophied.[1] The ineffeciency of centralisation and the costs of a local administrative vacuum, both revealed in the patent distress of numerous urban and rural areas, came to be recognised in the same period as debates about concerted national action on a new model suggested experimentation with a new localism.[2]

One result of this belated decentralisation was that the local partnerships were relatively free to choose and execute projects, and not subjected from the first, as in other countries, to reporting systems and centrally imposed guidelines that might have hampered their ability to manoeuvre freely. Another consequence was that local economic development and local provision of social welfare came to be seen as closely connected, if only because the central government's efforts to achieve both ends by distinct means was demonstrably inadequate. Areas of public action that in many other countries remain operationally distinct because of the vitality of public administrations with set and potentially competing jurisdictions thus came to be treated together in the experimental setting of the partnerships.

The long-standing Irish attachment to centralised administration meant also that, by the time they were finally given a chance, the local initiatives enjoyed unusually propitious economic conditions. In countries as different as the USA and Denmark or Sweden, efforts at administrative decentralisation are years and, in some instances, even decades old. They often predate the great waves of decentralisation within and among private enterprises that have been reshaping the OECD economies with gathering force since the mid-1970s. Hence, the notions of administrative efficiency, organisation of the labour market and definition of skill itself assumed by public authorities in their own reform deliberations in these countries were stamped with the impress of the great corporations of those mid-century days, and in large measure have continued to be so even though the original stamp may bear a new image. Beginning later, and entrusting greater discretion to local participants in touch with current economic developments, the Irish reforms have, effectively introduced, through the organising instrument of partnership, an ensemble of expectations about what the "modern" firm should look like and the skills necessary to build and work in one. These reforms suggest untried ways of joining training, job creation, and even rebuilding confidence undermined by long spells of joblessness.

Thus, partly because of their confidence in traditional community strengths and the possibility of mutual self-renewal, and partly as the accidental result of giving free administrative rein to local groups under current economic conditions, the Irish initiatives, by separate yet often convergent routes, have happened upon a master idea: to apply the problem-solving techniques of work teams now being disseminated throughout the OECD economies to simultaneously increase the self-reliance of the vulnerable – be they individuals, going firms, or start-ups – and to provide them with skills increasingly regarded as necessary for employment in jobs and industries with a future. We do not claim that this is the explicit and authoritative programme of the partnerships, nor, still less, that all of their experience can be subsumed under it, or even that, explicit or not, this programme is unique to Ireland. But we do claim that for the reasons just given, this outcome has begun to emerge with a speed and clarity of purpose in operation that is distinct from other efforts in the OECD to reform and connect economic development and welfare provision.

The Irish experience demonstrates that the principles guiding current economic restructuring contain the means for addressing some of the dislocations that restructuring itself causes, and especially for combining active, decentralised participation and the achievement of autonomy. Those who hope and those who despair that public action can in some measure counter the growing division in our societies between the accomplished and those lagging behind should therefore be equally attentive to the achievements and shortcomings of the Irish innovations.

STRUCTURE OF THE REPORT

Pessimism and progress in the Irish economy

Because the Irish reforms are comprehensive – taking up and trying to tie together diverse strands of national experience – our discussion of the experiments must likewise treat them in relation to the society as a whole: what it was when the reforms began, what it may become through their functioning. We begin in Chapter 2 by tracing the recent and surprising development of the Irish economy. The story of that economy is traditionally told as debility piled on debility. Ireland was weakened by centuries of colonial domination, to such an extent that it was unable to enjoy the advantages of late-developing countries either at the end of the nineteenth century, after independence or, later, upon entry into the European Union. The long-standing and continuing emblems of this debility are high rates of emigration and unemployment (and now, particularly, long-term unemployment); its current manifestation in the organisation of the economy is the division between a seemingly uncompetitive, vulnerable domestic sector and a high-performance multinational sector dominated by footloose firms ready to pull up stakes if the tax advantages that lured them to Ireland are trumped by a more appealing offer to relocate. The pessimism intrinsic to this view, we will argue, obscures a fundamental and extensive revitalisation of the Irish economy: a group of domestic firms that survived the earlier competition is becoming internationally competitive itself, and many of the multinationals are developing strong and apparently enduring ties with local suppliers, thus reducing the chance of further wandering.

The common denominator in both developments is the spread in ireland of innovative techniques of decentralised production originated by the Japanese and introduced to the country in altered form by US firms trying to master the new methods themselves. These techniques and the understanding of the economy on which they rest are, we will argue, on the way to becoming a *lingua franca* in dealings within and among more and more Irish firms, and in the process shaping the ways in which actors in parts of the public administration, and especially in the local partnerships, conceive economic problems. In support of these claims, we will draw on a recent review of the most current writings by academic observers, business consultants, and government officials on the restructuring of the Irish economy. Although this evidence furnishes the backdrop of our study and will accordingly be presented in summary form, this review was nonetheless prompted by the difficulty experts on the Irish economy have in reconciling the discrepancy between the apparent pervasiveness of knowledge of new organisational methods suggested by our initial findings and their own view of Ireland as a marginal participant to this day in the changes taking place abroad. Evidence of renewal that challenges the view of the economy as stagnant or fundamentally flawed does not, of course, validate the contrary idea that the country has entered an era of self-sustaining prosperity. But it is sufficient and necessary to explain how the partnerships could find their way so quickly to solutions that draw on techniques still regarded as experimental in many large firms. In addition, this evidence is a palpable confirmation that local actors have an understanding of these developments that is sometimes more current and settled in its orientation than that of experts at the centre.

Extending social partnership to the local level

Chapter 3 treats the origins of the partnerships in view of the paradoxical realisation by actors at the centre of government itself – particularly the Department of the Taoiseach or Prime Minister and the national unions – that they could broaden the limits of their directive capacities by decentralising authority. They came to this conclusion after recognising that economic stabilisation and the growth it made possible could not alone improve the life prospects of the most vulnerable groups, and, further, that the then-current combination of centralised economic development and welfare programmes could not accomplish what growth through concerted stabilisation could. This two-fold crisis in development and welfare policy then prompted a search for alternatives that led quickly to the discovery of novel, local forms of public-private partnership – some growing out of EU programmes in rural areas, others out of the immediate political concerns of the social partners themselves – as the institutional vehicle for escaping the blockages at the centre.

In detail, the beginnings of the partnerships in the efforts of the centre itself, the confusing profusion of new domestic and Community social-welfare and economic-development programmes as well as the concern of a beleaguered executive to maintain order while encouraging change are of course particular to Ireland. But readers of this report are likely to recognise in the confusion of initiatives, each a product at least as much of accident as plan, and the urge for a minimum of orderliness if not stability conditions that they know well from their own country. If so, they are likely to conclude further that there is nothing necessarily and restrictively Irish about the solutions discussed here because nothing uniquely rooted in the national past characterises their ingredient programmes and institutions. Thus we argue that the stream of Irish experience is connected to the larger flows of our day as much by the restless building up and tearing down of administrative structures and programmes in the search for some new and stable arrangement as by the character of its economic restructuring.

Projects and partnerships: transforming the local context

The account of project activities by local development groups (Chapter 4) is the core of the report. This section shows how in areas as diverse as the creation of new enterprises, vocational training and the organisation of assistance to established small firms, solutions reflect common themes directly tied to new principles of organisation: decentralisation of authority to small groups (ultimately work teams) with responsibility for results; regular review of the groups' efforts; and revision, in the light of this review, of both the original goals and the organisational means adopted for pursuing them. We will try to show that both the substance of the projects – the kinds of firms they aim to establish or whose adjustment they support, the kind of skills they teach and the way they teach them and the organisation of the partnerships, or parts of them, in relation to individual projects – are informed by these principles.

We have not undertaken anything like a formal evaluation of these projects in the conventional sense of attempting to estimate their influence on intended beneficiaries in comparison to a control group. However, the evidence presented suggests strongly that some element of the organisation and approach taken by local partnerships permits and encourages innovation in both social and economic programme design.

By their very nature, the kinds of innovations on view invite a searching and revealing form of inquiry that quickly exposes the limits and indicates the potential of a project. If groups of workers are being taught to solve problems by working as teams in industrial production, then the teaching method has failed if those groups cannot identify problems in the flow of the work they do. If they can identify problems, but cannot explain how they overcame them, then the instruction has failed midway towards its goal.

Judged by these and related tests, the projects described below are successful. If the problem-solving disciplines they impart are as fundamental to the economic vitality of individuals and firms under current conditions as we suppose, then projects that pass such tests are likely to contribute to the success of communities and whole economies according to some more encompassing accounting measures than we can contemplate here.

The project of "democratic experimentalism"

By way of conclusion, we gauge the partnerships' ability to assess themselves and learn – in a way available to state agencies – from one another's success and failure. As suggested at the outset, the conclusions in this regard are disappointing: although many of the experiments are successes, not all are. And it is hard to see how those in authority will be able to distinguish the two and learn from the exemplary cases as they do not appear to be systematically monitoring the results. But this defect, we will argue, is not incurable: on the contrary, by applying to the assessment of project results the same methods of disciplined self-evaluation that the projects are teaching their participants, public authorities can learn from the innovations they have spurred. We call monitoring of this type "democratic experimentalism" and we will argue that it can make the projects and partnerships accountable to their local constituencies and the polity as a whole in a way that provides an interim answer to the questions of administrative and democratic legitimacy raised by their exceptional status and can, in the long run, guide the development of Ireland's novel form of social partnership.

PESSIMISM AND PROGRESS
IN THE IRISH ECONOMY

INTRODUCTION

Underlying the evolution of local development initiatives in Ireland are processes of change within the Irish economy. Despite a period of relatively sustained economic growth over the past ten years, there is a lingering pessimism among Irish commentators about the ability of the Irish economy, outside the foreign multinational sector, to adapt to changing circumstances in the world economy and maintain a competitive position. This chapter looks at how this pessimism developed and, by invoking evidence of the introduction of new work practices and organisational techniques, shows why it is no longer satisfactory as an explanation of the condition of Irish industry. The full impact of adjustments within the private sector on Ireland's overall competitiveness are not clear, nor are adjustments that economic modernisation will provoke in broader aspects of public life and administration. However, the somewhat blurred picture emerging in the former setting starts to suggest the forms that will become apparent in the latter.

THE TRADITIONAL VIEW

Irish economic history, particularly as seen from Ireland, has been a story of vulnerability originating in foreign domination and propagated by the nation's own sincere but unsuccessful efforts to correct the earlier damage. As history, the story is accurate as far as it goes. But told and retold, it became a homily about limits to the economic capacities of the Irish, foretelling a future that compounded the mistakes of the past. As homily, the history kept even those most actively working to further the economy from identifying the possibilities created by current, partial successes. This chapter reviews this history and how its homiletic features were fixed in two influential, quasi-official reports on the Irish economy. It then characterises the current innovations in economic organisation which, extrapolating from those reports, ought to be beyond Irish reach, and presents evidence that many sectors of the Irish economy *are* coming to grips with the new methods, demonstrating capacities that belie the established account.

In the standard account, Ireland enters its modern economic history as a less-developed or underdeveloped country with little industry.[3] In the 1920s, only 13 per cent of the work force was employed in all of industry (manufacturing plus construction, power generation and distribution of electricity and gas), while the share so employed was about twice as large in comparable small European countries such as Denmark, Sweden, or the Netherlands.[4] One explanation for this retarded industrialisation is Ireland's position as a "capitalist colony" of Great Britain.[5] The British limited the expansion of Irish industry and encouraged its export-based agriculture in order to secure, on the one hand, a ready market for its own manufactured goods and, on the other, a cheap source of foodstuffs. Given high birth rates, one consequence was high rates of emigration. This in turn may have further distorted development by orienting the survival strategies of large groups in the population to the possibility of earning enough abroad to maintain possession of small rural holdings at home. Alternatively, the economic and political instability before independence encouraged a "possession mentality" among those who stayed in Ireland which inhibited the development of a "performance ethic". Either way, an attachment to traditional ways was fostered, in contrast to the notions of industrialisation that were being embraced elsewhere.[6]

It is consistent with this view of Ireland in the grip of foreign powers that manufacturing there (as in Brazil and Argentina, about which similar arguments are made) expanded following independence, particularly in the aftermath of the Great Depression when the international trade regime was in shards, foreign firms withdrew to their home markets, and domestic industry was protected by high tariff barriers. Autarky and the state intervention required to enforce it were both embraced with particular fervour in Ireland as it sought to extend and complete the creation of the independent Irish state that had been established only in 1923, not least to assert national economic autonomy.[7] Under the autarkic regime begun in the 1930s, the share of employment in industry as a whole increased to 22 per cent, below comparable European levels but about equal to that of the advanced developing countries of the day in Latin America. Expansion occurred in the production of consumer goods and less technologically demanding intermediate products: just those sectors where it is traditionally easiest to substitute domestic products for imports.

But as in comparable settings elsewhere, this growth soon proved to be of a hothouse variety. Irish manufactured goods were not competitive on world markets: only 6 per cent of manufactured output was exported in 1951 if products of the food, drink and tobacco industries are excluded from this category, and only 16 per cent if they are not. At the same time, the economy had reached a limit in its capacity to substitute imported capital goods with domestic equipment. Expansions in output, therefore, could only be achieved by importing machinery; but with exports stagnant, the Irish economy could not earn the foreign exchange needed to pay for the necessary imports. As in other countries reaching the limits of the protectionist import-substitution strategy, there soon followed balance-of-payment difficulties, and with them the corrective measures that redress the balances in the short-term by reducing domestic demand, employment, and growth.

In 1958, Irish policy makers, perceiving a reaction to the limits of import substitution later common in Latin America, did an about face, opening the economy to international competition and enticing foreign firms to locate in the country with the promise of a corporate tax on profits, not income, and at a low, flat rate. A free-trade agreement was signed with Great Britain in the mid-1960s, and free trade was established with the EC after Ireland became a member in 1973.

Although the early returns on this strategy were promising, by the end of the 1980s it appeared that openness had created debilitating divisions within the Irish economy and, worse still, paradoxically had helped recreate something akin to the very dependence on foreign economic power that "independence and autarky" had been intended to redress. Manufacturing output, which grew by only 1.7 per cent annually between 1951 and 1958, grew at 6.7 per cent per year between 1958 and 1973, 5.1 per cent annually during the next six years, and 6.6 per cent annually during the 1980s. For the period 1980 to 1991, growth in manufacturing output in Ireland at 6.6 per cent far outstripped that in any other OECD country, with Japan having the second best record at 4.2 per cent and the OECD average just 2.5 per cent.[8] Manufacturing employment grew rapidly, at least at the start of the new strategy, as well: the annual rate of increase jumped from 0.2 per cent in 1951-58 to 2.4 per cent from 1958-73, before falling back to 0.8 per cent in 1973-79.[9]

But signs of potential limits to the new strategy soon appeared, and became more visible as the years passed. When free trade started in earnest in the mid-1960s, domestic industry was quickly pushed aside by new entrants, particularly in those sectors where the latter were larger than domestic firms and therefore could take advantage of superior economies of scale. Irish firms continued to do well only in areas where "local" status conferred some commercial advantage, such as printing and foodstuffs. Employment in domestic firms stagnated from the mid-1960s to the end of the 1970s; in the next decade, when their loss of market share was no longer compensated for by growth in domestic demand, employment fell vertiginously – 27 per cent in seven years.

The foreign firms that relocated operations to Ireland generally did benefit from economies of scale. Had they been fully integrated into the Irish economy, therefore, they might have helped domestic firms overcome their weaknesses, for example, by supplying large and expanding markets to local suppliers who could in time achieve economies of scale themselves. But the kinds of firms attracted to Ireland were initially uninterested in these kinds of connections and did not work to establish them.

The first arrivals, who came in the 1960s, were units of multinationals in mature industries such as clothing and shoes; and the new entities, in effect internal subcontractors themselves, had no substantial need for local subcontractors of their own. Although (mostly American) firms in advanced sectors such as electronics, pharmaceuticals, medical instruments and machinery arrived in the 1970s, their participation in the local economy was likewise limited. The units they established in Ireland tended to engage in less technologically demanding activities such as assembly. Even when they were in technologically exigent lines of work, they appeared to get by without much exchange with the local economy. While the output of the foreign-owned firms and their share of total exports soared, measurement of the increase is complicated by the favourable corporate profit tax induced firms to transfer internally produced components to their Irish subsidiaries at low prices, thus artificially increasing the profitability of those units and reducing the corporation's overall tax bill.[10] On paper, output and productivity in multinational corporations (MNCs) doubled in the period 1987-93, constituting 40 per cent of the overall growth in national income during the period. But the productivity difference between the top-ten MNCs and the top-ten indigenous Irish firms is almost too striking to be plausible. Average output per employee for the best performing Irish companies in the period was Ir£ 128 000 in 1993, whereas for the ten most profitable foreign-owned companies it was Ir£ 814 000. According to Shirlow, the disparity between the two cannot be accounted for purely by higher capital intensity or superior management techniques within the MNC sector. Rather, he asserts that "the extremes of capital transfer pricing compose the central reason for the recorded differences in performance between Irish-owned companies and MNCs."[11]

In any case, whatever the true level of output and productivity growth, employment in the sector could not keep pace with the growth of the labour force. The difficulties the parent companies faced from Japanese and other competition in their home (American) market and the fears of imminent retreat from Ireland that news of these troubles aroused only reinforced the view that the Irish economy, weakened by competition from larger, more competitive firms, was connected to the world economy in a tenuous way that obstructed progress.

This view of the structural weakness of the Irish economy was officialised in two widely noted reports commissioned by the government. Both continue to serve today, often explicitly, as the framework for discussion of the shortcomings and possibilities of development. The first was the Telesis Report, prepared by the eponymous US consulting firm in 1982. Its central proposition was that inward investment had never succeeded as a long-term development strategy anywhere, and despite Ireland's better than average success in attracting foreign direct investment, neither would it work there.

According to the report, the fundamental weakness in the strategy was the disinclination on the part of multinationals to build ties to local firms and the propensity to disinvest when a more profitable production location appeared. Thus, the government's effective control of industrial policy was weakened by the policy itself. Reliable growth would have to come from the domestic sector, the report concluded, complemented by a much more *selective* attraction of foreign firms. The focus of industrial policy would have to shift accordingly. But it would be misguided, the argument continued, merely to redirect capital grants from multinationals to indigenous firms. The latter were too small and insufficiently innovative to compete with large firms enjoying economies of scale or established niche producers making specialised products. Indigenous firms, moreover, lacked the research and product development capacities with whose help they might, given the necessary investment funds, enter new markets. Moreover, they lacked the management capacity to remove the bottlenecks to innovation. To overcome these obstacles, the report concluded, it would be necessary to create a limited number of internationally competitive firms able to achieve economies of scale in key sectors. Expansion of these national champions would then animate the development of the rest of the indigenous sector.

Following such promptings, the government responded by directing the Industrial Development Agency (IDA), originally founded to attract foreign firms, to organise a range of programmes to improve the competitiveness of indigenous enterprises. The two major programmes established in the aftermath of Telesis were the Company Development Programme to assist strong, ambitious indigenous Irish enterprises, and the National Linkage Programme to assist potential or actual suppliers or subcontractors of multinational firms. Early optimism about the range of initiatives introduced by the IDA during this period was, however, short-lived. In 1992, the report of the Industrial Policy Review Group, otherwise known as the Culliton Report, confirmed the continued existence of the problems outlined by Telesis, noting, for (an extreme) example, that the office-machine sector sourced only 2 per cent of its industrial input needs domestically. Looking back at the policy failures of previous decades, however, the authors of the report were less sanguine about the effectiveness of national champions – even assuming they could be built through the use of government incentives and penalties – as instruments for improving the economy as a whole, and particularly the situation of the most vulnerable.[12]

This view, to repeat, is right as far as it goes. The period of autarky did not produce Irish firms so adept at mass production that they could compete with the multinational corporations that dominated the world economy up until the 1980s. Nor did autarky nurture niche producers who might have competed by producing high-quality speciality goods. Efforts to domesticate foreign mass producers or create national champions failed too. The results were obvious and obviously worrisome. Statistically recorded growth was not paralleled by a significant rise in living standards or improved employment conditions. For example, during the period 1987 to 1993, GNP grew at a yearly average of 4.7 per cent, while the volume of retail sales increased by a mere 1.9 per cent per annum, which, even taking into account the correction of public finances and an increase in saving, suggests that the rise in consumption lagged somewhat behind growth in national income.[13]

Unemployment, which fell from the onset of market opening in 1958 until 1974, started to rise because of retrenchment in the domestic sector and then stagnation in multinational hiring. The relatively small increases in unemployment between 1975 and 1980 became much more significant in the period 1980-87, during which time the rate more than doubled from 7.3 per cent to 17.6 per cent. After a slight recovery between 1987 and 1990, the upward trend became even more pronounced in the early 1990s, especially as regards long-term unemployment.[14] The apparent decoupling of economic growth and employment growth, and the increasing use of the term "jobless growth" to describe Ireland's situation, only added to the existing layers of pessimism.

Yet, whatever the virtues of this view as an explanation of failure, it became more and more misleading as a guide to success, and even as an account of actual developments. From the mid-1970s on, as Ireland was failing to build a mass-production economy, that model of economic organisation was being out-competed by new, more decentralised and flexible forms. Having come through experience to assume that modernisation requires mass production, the Irish were not alert to these larger changes in the definition of economic modernity. For the same reason, they were inattentive to the increasing, and increasingly successful, efforts of firms both in the domestic and foreign-owned sectors to adjust to these changes by adopting the new methods of organisation. Thus, confusion about the goal of development soon led to confusion, and undue pessimism, about the ability of the economy to progress at all. To see what the official view leaves out, and what the partnerships in their immediate contacts with the economy, are introducing into the picture of development, we will have to step back from the Irish story momentarily in order to say a word about changes in the understanding of efficiency that overtook the mass-production model, even as Ireland was trying to catch up with its successful practitioners.

DECENTRALISED PRODUCTION

The master principle of the old Taylorist system, we suggested above, was economies of scale. Efficiency was achieved by having a superintendent with comprehensive knowledge of market possibilities and production techniques design the product and subdivide its production into highly specialised, and, therefore, highly productive tasks, many of which could ultimately be simplified enough to be automated completely. The immediate results were the separation of conception and execution, the centralisation of the former at the top of a corporate hierarchy, and the (vertical) integration of suppliers making parts for particular makes and models of products into the firms using their output.

The costs of design and its translation into detailed jobs and specialised machines could be amortised as long as the production runs were enormous. As markets became more turbulent, though, and the combination of fluctuations in the level of demand and changes in technology shortened product life cycles, those costs became oppressively burdensome.

The new economic organisation is a response to this dilemma. It lowers the costs of adjustment to volatile conditions by allowing re-integration of conception and execution through a particular, highly disciplined form of decentralisation of authority in the design and production of goods and services. Each activity is housed in a (semi-)autonomous unit. Autonomy allows the units to reduce the costs of solving problems in its area of specialisation for any one client by accumulating experience in solving related ones for others. The improvements in efficiency that result from this continuous exploration of variety are called economies of scope.

The basal unit of this form of organisation is the independent work group or project team. Regardless of its formal legal status, it has sufficient authority over its internal organisation and sufficient choice in the procurement of the goods and services upon which it relies as inputs to be able to determine for itself the best means to pursue its ends. The activities of these teams are co-ordinated by a system of integrated goal setting: an initial project – to build, say, a car – is determined by examination of the best models of the relevant models currently available, and evaluation of likely developmental prospects. General specifications arrived at in this way are then repeatedly decomposed, again by reference to best practice and potential developments, into projects suited to single teams. As each team tries to realise its objectives, it suggests modifications in the initial design; cumulatively, these revisions in the design of the parts can lead to changes in the characterisation of the whole, and vice versa. The continuous re-evaluation and revision of the design, moreover, goes hand-in-hand with continuous re-evaluation and revision of the organisation dedicated to realising it, as difficulties in obtaining particular ends may reveal incorrect disposition of the means as well as shortcomings in the goals themselves. The same interpenetrating evaluation of means and ends, finally, guides production as well as design through the use of disciplines that detect and force immediate correction of the sources of defects either through re-organisation or re-design.[15]

These activities create a web of continuous comparisons which link and define the units collaborating in production. Benchmarking, for instance, is just the decomposition of competitors' products (or production processes) into their constituent elements and the synthesis of the elements that stand out as a result of the comparison into the prototype for a new design or process. Simultaneous or concurrent engineering is the practice of proceeding with the design of all components at once, rather than fixing the features of the most crucial parts in the order of their assumed importance, and using their definition as a frame for the rest. It uses comparison of the solutions that emerge from each partial elaboration of the original design to suggest and correct solutions to problems arising in connection with treatment of the others.[16]

Similar methods of comparison are used to order production itself. As designs are (provisionally) fixed, for example, suppliers and customers agree on target prices for components. These include annual or semi-annual price decreases to account for the gains in productivity expected to result from experience, as well as provisions for the division among the parties of gains in excess of the targets. Thus the parties expect to be continuously comparing target and actual performance and adjusting their expectations regarding future projects accordingly.[17] Finally, as the last bulwark against the encrustation of habit and the metaphor for the operating logic of the system as a whole, there is just-in-time or zero-inventory production. By removing the inventory buffers between work stations, this method assures that defects are detected and their source eliminated as soon as they are produced: a fault introduced at one work station obstructs operations as it is passed to the next, and discussion of how to fix the immediate problem is inextricably connected to discussion of how to prevent its recurrence by improving the equipment or proce- dure that produced it. Just-in-time production provides, therefore, a means of comparing the actual performance of a production system to the ideal of a system that operates error-free; and once any particular system has been stabilised at a given level of performance, it is sufficient to increase the demands on its reliabil- ity – for instance, by speeding up production – to reveal the currently most unrelia- ble or error-prone operations.

Operating together, these new disciplines overturn the verities of the earlier mass-production system, transforming the competing desiderata of that world into mutually reinforcing attributes of the new one. Thus, in mass-production a decrease in efficiency was the price for an increase in quality. Greater attention to accuracy inevitably seemed to reduce the throughput of the system per unit time, and thus to decrease its productivity. But the new system's increasing demands on quality are used to reveal defects in the organisation of production that would have remained hidden under less exigent conditions; and correction of these defects cumulatively reveals possibilities for raising efficiency – through minimising downtime due to repairs, through the introduction of delicate automation equipment whose opera- tion depends on maintenance of tight tolerances, through reduction in the rework of botched products – unavailable in an environment more tolerant of fault. Similarly, it counted as a truism of the older methods that exploration of many design alternatives hindered timely and rigorous pursuit of any one. Simultaneous engi- neering shows that pursuit of many alternatives is the best way of understanding the advantages or disadvantages of each; so exploration of many contributes to selection of the best of current possibilities.

All these changes place new demands on the firm's principal collaborators: suppliers providing components or services and employees providing skills. In mass production, suppliers worked using blueprints and often utilised machinery designed or even directly provided by the customer. Suppliers competed with each other on price; how they met their contractual promises was their business. But once production is truly collaborative, final producers need to know not just that suppliers can meet price targets, but also if they can improve designs and production set-ups in co-operation with others. As the bid is effectively a promise to do something the supplier has never, in that precise form, done before, and which the customer alone cannot do or even fully define, a bid that meets the target price is meaningless unless accompanied by a credible assessment of the supplier's capacity to do as promised.

Such assessments are provided in a publicly accessible form by certification under a new type of international standard. Unlike conventional standards, they specify neither the characteristics of products nor features of production processes – nor do they even prescribe methods for documenting the latter. What they do instead is establish procedures by which firms can be certified as warranted to make claims regarding their capability to perform as promised. Under the most comprehensive and widely acknowledged of these standards, the ISO 9 000 series maintained by the International Organisation for Standardisation in Geneva, Switzerland, a production facility is certified as capable of designing and delivering products and services to customers' requirements in all areas of economic endeavour. To obtain certification a firm must convince a registrar (whose authority derives from association with the standard-maintaining body) that it can register customer expectations or detect performance shortfalls. At a minimum, it must be in control of operations to such an extent that it can document what it does, and do what the documents say. In theory, the ISO standards do not require firms to adopt any particular technology, form of organisation or procedures at all, although in practice some ends can be obtained by such limited means that to pursue them narrowly determines operational choices. Nor does it replace detailed discussion of individual projects or of the performance measures to evaluate them. Certification does qualify a firm as a reliable interlocutor in eventual discussion about its performance capacities. It also establishes that collaborators are likely to understand one another's assertions because they can assume common understanding of the criteria by which such assertions can be justified. The language of certification is thus the language in which projects are discussed, and the diffusion of this language is thus a sign and precondition of the spread of the new methods.

The transformation of skill in the new system is subtler and harder to fix in standards, but no less thoroughgoing. In mass production, skills were of two kinds.

Either they were concerned with machine tending and thus so narrow and so specific to particular firms or machines that they had to be learned on the job. The great majority of workers in mass-production firms started out doing the most menial of such jobs, and became semiskilled as they progressed up a job ladder of related, successively more demanding tasks as experience permitted, or the skills were of a craft character; craft skill is the ability to combine theoretical and practical knowledge of a related body of tools, materials, and techniques to solve complex, often incompletely specified tasks with only indicative instructions. Because craft workers define their own tasks, given general indications of the goal, they can build and maintain the specialised machines on which mass production depends.

The skills of employees in the work teams of the new collaborative production fit neither category: their activities are farther ranging, more varied, and more dependent on the exercise of autonomy than those of the semiskilled worker. But, precisely because they are so mutable, they do not originate in, nor are they fixed by, the mastery of particular tools, materials, or techniques characteristic of craft work. Their knowledge is a distinctive kind that blends attention to technical detail, features of the group itself and its members, and the organisations to which these are connected. Their master skill is the ability to solve problems in groups, where the reorganisation of the group and its relation to other groups can be part of the solution. In the US, persons with this skill are frequently – if imprecisely – called technicians. Their defining characteristic is the ability to combine the skills used to manipulate tools and machines typical of the manual worker with the organisa-tional abilities of the manager and the capacity to bring abstractions to bear in the resolution of clinical problems associated with the professional; and they are the fastest growing category in the census of occupations.

Bufferless production systems and collaborative supply arrangements have been diffusing to the United States, Great Britain and Southeast Asia from Japan via transplants since the mid-1980s, and from the US to Western Europe and much of Latin America more recently. But this current wave of innovation seemed to pass Ireland by. How could it be otherwise? Ireland, in the standard view, was backward because it was subordinated to the world economy in a way tantamount to isola-tion. And how could an isolated country stay abreast of the most advanced developments?

Had the assumption of subordination been correct, then the conclusion would be too. But as is discussed next, contrary to conventional wisdom, the multinational and domestic sectors of the economy have begun to adopt the new methods extensively enough to change the categories within which the capacities of firms and the value of skills are assessed.

RECONSIDERING RECENT DEVELOPMENTS

Much of the adjustment in the practices of multinational and indigenous firms, evidence of which will be discussed below, is incremental. In many cases, firms embrace certain new techniques while retaining traditional methods in other areas. The true extent of the spread of new methods is therefore masked. Its impact on the competitiveness of individual Irish firms, or on the economy as a whole, is difficult to gauge. If the question asked is how much has changed definitively for the better, the answer is that in Ireland, as elsewhere, it is hard to say. However, if the question is how much has changed in the direction of the new methods, the answer for Ireland is a great deal. The full implications of these changes for the labour market and industrial relations, and for the institutions of government and social partners which defined themselves according to traditional categories, are also unclear, but it seems safe to assume that the impact is substantial.[18]

The best documented changes concern the foreign-owned sector, and particular Irish units of multinationals in industries such as computers and software, which are establishing collaborative relations with local suppliers and reorganising their internal operations accordingly. Leading examples are the Irish subsidiaries of Apple, Microsoft, Intel, and Amdahl. All are creating "strategic partnerships", in which the few suppliers who will eventually produce components of the final product are involved at early stages in its design and development. There are nuances: Amdahl insists that suppliers "should not focus too much on any one major customer". Diversification helps suppliers "maintain a high level of expertise through exposure to other technologies" and dependence on any one customer might damage both partners.[19] Microsoft, while also reducing the number of suppliers and building long-term relations with the remaining ones, does not, so far, insist on diversification.[20]

The fullest picture of the emerging relations between customer and supplier is furnished in a report on Apple. Its suppliers are described as "one-stop shops" capable of executing increasingly complex projects. Apple initially selects suppliers for their competence in a particular area of manufacturing. But capable suppliers are then asked to undertake or supervise activities complementary to the initial task. Thus, the plastic moulding company, Rennicks, was at first used only for moulding. By 1994, they were supplying to Apple "a complete assembly – plastics, sheet metal shields, inserts and heatstaking." Apple's strategy is to have "suppliers purchasing many subassemblies, drives, power supplies, etc., assembling the product and shipping a finished product to Apple for distribution". Working directly with Apple-approved suppliers, companies like BG Turnkey and Walsh Western themselves procure the manuals, software, keyboards, cables and warranty information supplied with the central processing unit of the computer itself, and ship these kits to Apple. Eventually, Apple plans to specify only the overall requirements for the kits and leave the selection of the supplier as well as responsibility for setting prices and managing quality to the "turnkey" assembler.[21] Firms with these capacities can presumably diversify their customer base if they want to. At the same time, these same capacities provide substantial autonomy in dealings with even the largest client, and thus may reduce the need, at least initially, to seek others. In either case, the new relation connects the multinational to the local economy in a way that connects the latter to world markets and the disciplines needed to compete in them.

These changes in turn are beginning to have repercussions within the small- and medium-sized sector of traditional domestic industry. The best-studied case is the software manual printing industry (SMPI) – consisting of a small number of SMEs and subsidiaries of Irish and American multinationals. It has grown rapidly since the mid-1980s as supplier/buyer alliances with the subsidiaries of multinational software companies like Microsoft and Symantec, and domestic firms invested substantially in advanced, product-specific printing machinery. Firms in the industry are moving into up-stream and downstream activities, either acting alone by forming new business units for this purpose, or by entering into alliances with other independent companies, including major customers. Here, too, concerns about continuing dependence on large, foreign customers is substantially offset by demonstrable increases in the capacities of the local suppliers.[22]

Developments at Avenue Mouldmaking in Dublin illustrate the potential reach of these changes. Avenue Mouldmaking supplies the Irish subsidiaries of a number of major multinationals. Its senior managers work closely with these companies, sometimes in formal problem solving groups. This brings them into contact with some of the most highly developed versions of production systems in Europe and the US. From these exchanges with its customers, Avenue has incorporated advanced budgeting practices as well as improvements in mould-making and, more generally, in the use of materials and production organisation. In some cases, the customer is in effect acting as go-between, obtaining best-practice information from a supplier with whom it operates and passing it on to others.[23] It is worth noting, too, that foreign capital is also introducing the new methods to the small- and medium-sized enterprise sector directly by buying or establishing small firms in Ireland, rather than through customer/supplier relations. The share of foreign-owned companies in the group of the most advanced small firms is substantially larger than the share owned by foreigners of all small firms in Ireland.[24]

But change in the domestic sector is hardly dependent on contact, direct or indirect, with foreign firms. Irish-owned companies in traditional sectors are beginning to adopt the new methods on their own initiative, often with help from an increasing number of private consulting firms and public agencies specialising in industrial adjustment. Leading examples are: Dublin Fine Meats;[25] Moffett Engineering in Monaghan, whose output nearly doubled in 1994 and whose rate of on-time deliveries was raised with little increase in inventory; Press-O-Matic, a refrigeration equipment manufacturer; APA Systems, a producer of aluminium and PVC doors in Dublin; CEL in Tuam, a supplier of vehicle security systems; Rye Valley Foods in Carrickmacross, a ready-meals manufacturer; and the Irish Co-op Society in Limerick, a manufacturer of corrugated packaging for food. This list suggests, and discussion among expert observers confirms, that food processing firms, a key component of the domestic manufacturing sector producing almost one-third of gross value added in Irish manufacturing, are on the verge of adopting the new methods.[26]

The profusion of consultancies, public and private, aiming to serve the nascent market for advice in introducing the new systems also suggests that this disposition is widespread. Besides Lucas Engineering & Systems, there are such names as IPC, the Western Management Centre, AMT, TMS Cork, PA, and a Manufacturing Consultancy Service operated by Forbairt, the state agency concerned with the development of domestic small firms.[27] In addition, the Services to Business Division of FÁS, the state training agency, is experimenting with a programme of assisting clusters of small firms in the same area in co-ordinating discussion of reorganisation. Ten companies in the same region are chosen and a panel of experts, with various functional specialities, is made available to the companies, each company having a total of up to 19 days of access to the panel over a year. The scheme is currently being piloted in three regions. Participating firms must have fewer than 50 employees, a turnover of under Ir£ 3 million and have been identified by FÁS as having management development needs.[28]

A survey of 98 firms that won the Q-mark Award in 1995 confirms that however far Irish firms may be from having a fully consolidated variant of the new-model corporation, they have broken with the practices associated with mass-production as the following figures show: twenty per cent of the respondents materially reward employees for customer service success; most firms have reduced the number of their suppliers over the last five years; price is an important criterion for approving suppliers for only 30 per cent of respondents; "86 per cent have required suppliers to be both more reliable in delivery and more flexible and responsive in both deliveries and deadlines in the past three years"; "as companies develop towards the 'best' customer service category, an increasing proportion will adopt TQM"; 45 per cent use JIT, and most of these have reduced their number of suppliers in the last three years. For most of the respondents, it would not be difficult for their customers to find alternative sources. To improve links with customers, 24 per cent have "interlocking computer systems" with major customers; another 30 per cent use one or more electronic notice boards, e-mail, and computerised invoicing and processing; 46 per cent use EDI, but mostly at the early stages; 66 per cent of respondents budget for innovation; 65 per cent have targets for percentage of turnover to be achieved by new products/services; customer-service is associated with innovation, but there is more evidence of individuals having responsibility for innovation than of everyone, at all levels, in all functions, pursuing innovation. Training is important at both management and non-management levels in most of the respondent companies, with expenditure on training – and on customer service training in particular – much higher than the Irish average. Most respondents also use a variety of "motivational tools", including autonomous work groups (16 per cent), profit sharing (23 per cent), quality circles (23 per cent), job enrichment (25 per cent), bonus schemes (40 per cent), financial disclosure (41 per cent), job rotation (45 per cent), performance appraisal (70 per cent).[29]

Little of this, to underscore a point made at the outset of this section, is visible from the vantage point of changes in industrial relations at the plant, as opposed to national, level. Local unions, according to the survey, are at the margins of events, and changes in the organisation of work, the flow of information in the firm, and even compensation methods, are often accomplished without their active participation:

> There is little evidence of the acceptance of the idea that unions have a role to play in the development, maintenance or evaluation of quality programmes and less than half the unionised companies involved unions in the imple-mentation of quality programmes.[30]

On the other hand, the quality initiatives had been accompanied by increasing sophistication in recruitment and selection, induction, performance appraisal and the use of employee involvement initiatives in half the companies. Performance-related pay systems had changed in 16 per cent of companies. Improved communi-cation as a result of the quality initiatives was reported by most respondents (81 per cent). This improvement was evident at and between all levels in the responding organisations.[31]

Compiling this evidence Irish observers are led to conclude that earlier and apparently overstated assessments by outsiders of the extent of renovation in the Irish economy may not be as far from the mark as their own habits of thought had originally suggested. Jacobson writes:

> Within and between firms, with the support of a number of public agencies, and the commitment and enthusiasm of the trade union movement, at least at the central level, new forms of work organisation are becoming more common. In comparative terms, the work of the European Foundation suggests that if Ireland's position is still roughly that of the late 1980s, it is in these respects at least ahead of the European average.[32]

Despite the encouragement of both government agencies and the social part-ners, a sufficiently widespread adoption of new models within firms raises ques-tions about the relevance of organisational structures and modes of thought based on an apparently declining, or at least less universal, model. The most obvious example is that of industrial relations, but most other arenas of public policy action are touched by the unsettling effect of changes in the nature and organisation of economic activity.

The next chapter looks at how threats to the effectiveness of central-level policy-making contributed first to the creation of a national social partnership arrangement and then to the transfer of the system to local institutions. These institutions are implicitly informed by changes in the economy and are an explicit attempt to deal with the instability they are provoking. The unusual element in the Irish response, and perhaps what gives it its particular force, is the promotion of experimentalism, rather than cautious conservatism, as a reaction to instability.

3

EXTENDING SOCIAL PARTNERSHIP
TO THE LOCAL LEVEL

The chief protagonists of the decentralisation of Irish public administration were actors at the centre of government itself, in particular the Department of the Taoiseach (Prime Minister's office) acting with the social partners, especially the national trade unions. These prime movers were activated at least as much by recognition of the limits of the centre's directive capacities as by a precise understanding of how local action could achieve what they could not. First, and most generally, they had come to realise that economic growth by itself would not improve the living conditions and prospects of the most vulnerable groups, and that existing centralised welfare programs could not accomplish what growth left unfinished. As part and parcel of this recognition, the architects of decentralisation acknowledged that social partnership between business and labour at the national level, however indispensable it was in addressing the nation's urgent macro-economic difficulties, could not guarantee the extension of the benefits of eventual prosperity to the long-term unemployed and other groups suffering from economic distress. By implication, even a policy of pursuing prosperity by placing concern for national equity at the centre of the debate would not be inclusionary enough to meet the needs of marginal groups. Finally, for reasons closely related to those at the origins of their doubts about the limited effectiveness of centralised administration and concerted national action (and encouraged in the same direction by changes in the guidelines for community funding), the reformers were disposed to look to novel, local forms of public-private partnership as the institutional vehicle for escaping the blockages at the centre.

The clearest, most direct expression of these concerns are the Area-Based Partnerships (ABPs), formed in 1991. They were created explicitly to address economic disintegration and its consequences (mainly in terms of unemployment)[33] and, as evidenced by their formal structure, implicitly to do so in a way that blurs familiar distinctions between public and private, national and local, representative democracy and direct participation in public affairs. As limited companies, subject to the Companies Act (1991), each must have a board of directors. It is in the composition and legal responsibilities of these boards that the unique ambiguities of the institution are evident. Typically, an Area-Based Partnership will have a board of 18 members, drawn in equal proportions from the "statutory agencies" (divisions or bureaux of the national government concerned with training or economic development), the "social partners" (trade unions, farmers and business associations), and the "community sector" (groups active in matters as diverse as welfare or tenant rights or crime-fighting). In practice, the state selects regional officials of agencies whose operation is of local concern, the social partners nominate local persons affiliated with their respective activities, and representatives of community groups are either elected or placed on boards in general recognition of their level of activity or public standing in the area. But original affiliations aside, all board members have under the Companies Act a primary responsibility to the partnership or "company" they direct, not the organisations that nominated them. Thus the ABPs are, by deliberate paradox, well-situated to exploit the resources of various national bureaucracies, the patronage of the social partners (including, for example, private sector businessmen active in employers associations), and the local political and substantive expertise of community groups – without being directly answerable to any of them. To the extent that they make use of these possibilities, the ABPs naturally become at least a complement to and perhaps a partial substitute for local government; yet they are not obliged to account for themselves to the latter either. Through the proposals they advance for changes in administrative or legislative norms, the imaginative recombination of existing local and national government programmes, and the novel enterprise-creation or training projects they authorise, the partnerships are engaging in the kind of participatory reform of established institutions that bypasses most formal democratic procedures.

In this chapter we show how dissatisfaction with the instruments of a centralised welfare system and understanding of the limits of traditional, national social-partnership could culminate in the creation of a new type of local social-partnership that is at once an extension of the machinery of the centre and, potentially, an autonomous mechanism for its reform. Then we take up the third and last of the foundational considerations, the idea of public-private partnerships, as it was articulated in the formation of entities such as the Pilot Area Programme for Integrated Rural Development (and subsequently LEADER) and the County Enterprise Boards. The earliest of these antedated the local partnerships, were animated by similar concerns, and in unobtrusive ways shaped the institutional understanding of partnership that informs the ABPs as well. So great are the affinities, indeed, that today all of these institutions seem to form a class. The work, just begun, of fitting each to the others and the whole group to more established institutions only underscores the unsettling differences between the new local experimentalism and the familiar principles of public administration, from which, in search of answers to urgent public problems, and with the encouragement of the centre itself, local groups have departed.

LIMITS TO CENTRALISED WELFARE POLICY: THE EXAMPLE OF HOUSING

Because of its striking combination of successes and failures, housing policy and its results came to be seen both as one of the chief symbols of the limits of centralised remedies to social problems and a kind of imaging device that revealed problems with similar endeavours in other arenas. By subsidising home ownership and spending substantial amounts of money on public housing, successive Irish governments made it possible by the late – 1980s for (almost) any family who could own a house to own one. Those who could not found accommodations instead on local authority estates whose housing stock was of better quality and design than that available in equivalent dwellings in many other countries.[34] Judged, therefore, by the material and psychological satisfaction that it provided to the majority, housing policy could fairly be counted a success.

At the same time, however, these policies unintentionally encouraged the geographical concentration of the poorest and economically most vulnerable households on particular housing estates, thus marking them off from the general population and casting them into a circumscribed environment where, as analogous experience in many countries shows, dejection and defeatism often become important enough to make hope of improvement seem like self-deception. The combination of subsidies to home ownership and good-quality public housing led, for example, to a decline in the availability of low-cost rental units. For lower-income families, the alternative to home ownership thus increasingly became occupancy in estate housing. This, together with social trends such as a rise in the number of single-parent households, led to a gradual decrease in the average income level of estate residents and, in some instances, to growing disparities between the best- and worst-off recipients of public housing. These disparities inside the overall group of public-housing residents were then translated into geographic separation by the introduction of transfer mechanisms which effectively moved the "good", long-established tenants to the most popular estates. This set in motion a game of "snakes and ladders", with the housing that was vacated being allocated to potential tenants lower down in the queue. As a result, the lowest quality and least desirable housing became occupied by the more marginalised and worst-off groups.

These sorting mechanisms were exacerbated by subtle design flaws in the estate-building policy and urban land-use zoning more generally. For one example, to keep construction costs down, the large-scale rehousing projects in the outlying suburbs were built *en bloc*, with units of the same type and size grouped together. The unanticipated consequence was that both smaller households (usually one-parent families) and larger ones (with several children) – precisely those statistically at greater risk of poverty – were separated out from the more prosperous and stable median-sized families. For another, maintenance costs, particularly of the "low-cost" housing built in the late 1960s and 1970s, are running higher than expected, and given the choice between expensive repairs or renovations on the one hand and preservation of low rents on the other, funding for public housing has been concentrated on the latter. Finally, the new suburbs were often undersupplied with such essentials of commercial infrastructure as shopping centres. Beyond the inconveniences this caused in daily life, it also resulted in an undersized employment base in the area and made the community more vulnerable to economic downturns than it otherwise could have been.

Finally, even as dilapidation made manifest the effects of sorting and separation, the pattern of industrial settlement throughout the 1970s set islands of increasing industrial activity next to the islands of increasing poverty in a archipelago of contrasts that could not help but call attention to the growing disparities in Irish society and the subtle ways that government policy at the centre involuntarily accentuated them. In the same period that the large housing estates were built on the outskirts of Dublin and other cities to house a growing population and ease the pressure on the congested city centres, the foreign enterprises being attracted to the country were often located nearby on specially built industrial estates or on greenfield sites. As individual mobility was also increasing within Irish labour markets and firms were becoming more selective in choosing employees, the new arrivals hardly limited their search for a workforce to the abutting neighbourhoods. On the contrary, they tended to look for their future employees in distant suburbs, and, for reasons we will examine in the next chapter, these initial decisions became self-reinforcing. Hence the apparent benefits of living near an industrial zone were rarely passed on to the local community. Today, as a result, it is commonplace to find a run-down housing estate with an extremely high long-term unemployment rate cheek-by-jowl with an industrial zone full of successful foreign and domestic medium-sized firms. Somehow, the same policies that brought prosperity to the very doorsteps of the poor could bring it no further, and by some perverse self-subversion even encouraged the beneficiaries of the new economic possibilities to look away from the apparently menacing portals just beyond their workplaces.[35] No wonder, then, that housing and housing policy can be seen not as a principal cause of social problems in Ireland, but rather, to repeat, as a symbol of the limits to the success of discrete central programmes.

Since the publication of the government housing policy statement "A Plan For Social Housing" in 1991, it has been a specific objective of government housing policy to mitigate the extent and effect of social segregation in housing. Local authorities are now legally required to draw up and adopt a written statement of their policy to counteract undue segregation in housing between people of different social backgrounds.

Local authorities are also encouraged to provide new housing in smaller developments and to avoid where possible adding to existing large-scale local authority housing estates. General guidance has been given to local authorities in regard to the size of new estates which would be appropriate in different circumstances and on the design and location of new schemes. Local authorities have also been requested to develop, as far as possible, infill sites for local authority housing allowing the new housing to be integrated into existing services and communities. Since 1991, local authorities are also increasingly meeting needs by purchasing existing houses where this represents reasonable value for money. As a result, the purchase of existing houses accounted for over 16% of the local authority housing programme in 1994 and 24% in 1995.

Local authorities are being encouraged to dispose of land which may no longer be suitable for new local authority housing due to the proximity of existing large public housing areas, and to purchase other more suitable land instead. Short or medium term loan finance is made available by the Housing Finance Agency for the purchase by local authorities of land for any of their housing functions. Adjoining local authorities are encouraged to co-ordinate their activities to ensure that land is used in a manner that avoids increased social segregation.

The diversification of social housing provision, notably the increased share being provided by the voluntary/non-profit sector and the shared ownership system, also helps counteract social segregation.[36]

CONCERTATION AND ITS LIMITS

If housing symbolised the importance of unintended consequences in limiting the impact of the centre's inclusionary policies, macroeconomic concerns forced explicit, public recognition that national co-ordination in a crucial arena could, in the absence of safeguards and countermeasures, actually come at the expense of significant groups within the society. The dilemma was this: by the mid-1980s, explosive growth of the public debt gave rise to credible fears that the Irish government could default on its obligations. The remedy was to restrict public and private consumption so as to increase the reserves available to satisfy creditors. These cutbacks, however, would normally burden marginal groups the most – those dependent on social welfare transfers and those at the bottom of the labour market with limited bargaining power. From the efforts to reconcile restraint with inclusion came first the idea of national social partnership and then, when its limits, too, became visible, the determination to decentralise authority over the definition of inclusionary policies to the affected areas and groups themselves.

At a decade's distance, it is sometimes hard for the Irish themselves to recall the urgency of the macroeconomic crisis of the mid-1980s.[37] Already, by the end of the 1970s, efforts to finance continued growth in the midst of international recession had increased public-sector borrowing to almost 16 per cent of GNP. The situation worsened after Ireland, in hopes of cutting its high inflation rate, joined the European Exchange Rate Mechanism (ERM) in 1979. The same fixed exchange rates that assured investors of the stability of the Irish punt also prohibited the government from boosting exports through devaluation. Thus in the period 1980 to 1987, the economy stagnated. Total employment fell by almost 6 per cent and manufacturing employment by 25 per cent. Living standards fell accordingly as the rate of unemployment increased from 7.1 per cent in 1979 to almost 18 per cent in 1987. But for a return to the traditionally high levels of emigration in the mid- and late-1980s, the outcome on the domestic labour market would have been substantially worse. By 1987, public debt was approaching 130 per cent of gross national product and insolvency was a menacing possibility.

Against this background, the social partners and the incoming government took the occasion to negotiate a three-year, tripartite Programme for National Recovery (PNR). Its defining feature, hinted at in a report published a year earlier by the National Economic and Social Council,[38] was an exchange between the national trade unions and the government: the unions agreed not only to accept reductions in public spending, but also to moderate wage demands as a means of restoring the international competitiveness of Irish goods and avoiding inflationary pressures that could undermine the stabilisation programme. For its part, the government guaranteed not to cut social welfare payments and to reform income tax to the benefit of employees. More generally, all parties to the agreement undertook to do nothing to generate inflationary pressures that might prompt calls for devaluation, nor to call for devaluation themselves if external problems arose. A new Central Review Committee (CRC) was to monitor implementation of the programme and ensure consultation among the government and the social partners on open questions.

From here it was, again with the benefit of hindsight, a short step to the creation of local partnerships. As a pick-up in growth rates and increases in manufacturing employment and exports gave early indications of what proved to be enduring success,[39] consideration turned to the possibility and conditions for extending the national agreement. Again, negotiation between the government and the social partners was inspired by their participation in an NESC analysis, this time the influential *Strategy for the Nineties,* which emphasised that long-term unemployment was the most critical policy issue and suggested local initiatives as a main policy response.[40] For participants in the CRC, especially the unions and the Department of the Taoiseach, extension appeared, paradoxically, to be as threatening to their institutional self-interest as it was necessary for their survival. On the one hand, as architects of the original agreement they could claim credit for having rallied the nation and having acted in – indeed, defined – the national interest. To abandon this success was therefore unlikely. On the other hand, the substance of the national recovery programme so limited their freedom of action that in supporting the general interest they could be accused of abandoning the particular concerns of the groups they represented. Their search for new fields of activity, consistent with the spirit of the agreement but appealing to their own constituencies, led each towards policies for the unemployed and socially excluded and then to the idea of extending the national bargain to include local development. Thus Section VII of the successor agreement to the PNR – renamed the Programme for Economic and Social Progress (PESP), signed in 1990 and running through 1993 – provided for the establishment of the Area-Based Response to Long-Term Unemployment and the creation of 12 pilot partnerships to combat unemployment in areas of particular disadvantage (the first ABPs). To each in its own way, the partnerships were a means of overcoming political instability.

For the unions, creation of the partnerships under the PESP was an opportunity to play the broader role that they had begun to take on in the 1980s. In part, this development was spurred by the attrition of heavily unionised indigenous industry and the increasing importance of multinational firms which were either not unionised or were covered by plant- or firm-specific agreements whose connection to the established body of collective bargaining agreements and practice was uncertain. To this constriction were added the new constraints of the macroeconomic environment: in exchanging a pledge of fiscal responsibility for a seat at the national bargaining table, the unions were also agreeing for a time to refrain from all but nominal wage bargaining. In these circumstances, they were anxious to find themes of broad interest to the labour force over which they *could* bargain. Given the high rates of unemployment among their members or their members' families and neighbours, and the even more widespread worries of job insecurity, programmes to improve job placement and combat impoverishment could be seen as partial compensation for the wage increases foregone by those in secure employment. One measure of the unions' interest in establishing their legitimacy in this regard is their creation in 1985 of Centres for the Unemployed. In fact, the area-based approach of these centres, of which there are now 29, foreshadowed the interest of the unions in decentralised partnership structures in the PESP negotiations. In making themselves the defenders of the unemployed, the unions could justifiably portray themselves in the PESP negotiations as the representatives of a general interest, not advocates of privileged groups.

As part of its normal functions, it fell naturally upon the Department of the Taoiseach to lead negotiations on the PESP and thereby to assume responsbility for the implementation of the local partnership scheme. Nevertheless, the creation of the partnerships afforded an opportunity for it to secure a measure of influence over the administrative apparatus formally under its control. The Department of the Taoiseach, like its homologues elsewhere, is designed to assure a certain margin of manœuvre for the prime minister in dealing not only with the legislature but also, and perhaps above all, with a public administration divided into traditional functional departments forced to compete for dwindling resources. From this perspective, the widespread public acknowledgement of the shortcomings of the government's centralised housing, social welfare, and economic development policies gave the Department of the Taoiseach an unusually advantageous occasion to make itself the catalyst of administrative reform. By providing that local representatives of the state development and training agencies sit on the partnership boards, the department became the sponsor of *de facto*, experimental integration of services without having to elaborate plans for reform and defend them against the well-informed, but perhaps self-interested objections of the concerned departments. This relaxation of the normal procedures of reform raises, of course, serious questions of accountability; for that and other reasons, as we will see in Chapter 5, it is already under attack. But as a device to break the log-jam of administrative reorganisation and to establish the Department of the Taoiseach as a catalyst of local self-determination, the strategy of bringing the lower levels of the specialised bureaucracies into the area-based partnership structure was highly effective.

Those familiar with tripartite, neo-corporatist arrangements in, for example, Austria or the Nordic countries will remark how unusual both the background conditions and outcome of these Irish developments appear when compared to these earlier and better-known forms of social partnership. In these more familiar cases, a strong, even dominant social-democratic party is often taken as a precondition for inclusionary macroeconomic policies. But Ireland has no such party. This leaves the possibility, as in countries such as Japan and Switzerland which likewise lack strong social democratic tradition, that the origins of solidarity lie in a diffuse, historically determined culture of cohesion and consensus-building. But for Ireland, at least, this explanation is also unsatisfying because it overlooks the unsuccessful attempts at national agreements in the years between 1970 and 1981. This period gave so few indications of the social consensus that was to follow that an influential commentator wrote in 1988 that the chances of an inclusionary bargaining agreement in Ireland were slim.[41] For the moment, therefore, the origins of social partnership arrangement fit uneasily into standard explanations. Whether this is because they are a singular exception *sui generis*, or because they are an early instance of a type of social partnership reachable under current economic and social conditions from many starting points and, as such, destined to become widespread, only time will tell.

The same is true for the substance of Irish social partnership. In the familiar neo-corporatist arrangements, the opening of markets and acceptance of fixed exchange rates typically went hand in hand with the creation of an extensive and elaborate system of internal transfers – from consumers to producers, from export industry to domestic agriculture – whose purpose was to buffer vulnerable sectors from the effects of world market competition. In Austria, to take a well-known example, the Schilling has been pegged to the German DM for more than a decade and, until recently, disadvantaged groups were protected either through the use of state-owned firms or non-tariff barriers to competition (for, example, a mutual non-competition agreement between Austrian and German banks). Welfare transfers (particularly, in the Austrian case, in the form of early-retirement benefits to skilled workers dislocated by industrial reorganisation) are, of course, an integral part of these compensatory systems. As such they must be administered from the centre to ensure roughly equal treatment of social groups under changing conditions. In practice, the long-term result of these systems is to create a web of bargains and entitlements whose bewildering complexity limits the possibilities of public action while raising among the citizens the suspicion that the beneficiaries of public spending are selected by political influence, if not by chance.

The new Irish social partnership – or "concertation", to use the term adopted in part to make this very point – deliberately differs from this pattern. First, it limits the provision of anything like comprehensive social insurance to the most vulnerable groups – the poor and the unemployed – instead of extending implicit guarantees of security to whole sectors or subsectors of the economy.[42] So spare are the guarantees, indeed, that some observers have dismissed concertation as nothing but a fig leaf covering retrenchment in the name of fiscal stabilisation. But this assertion ignores the substantial government commitments to maintain the welfare and health-provision system.

The second distinctive difference of Irish concertation is in many ways a consequence of the first. By limiting the possibilities of compensating groups through transfers or adjustment policies orchestrated at the centre, concertation obliges the actors to look to innovations in structural policy in general, and local innovations in particular, to protect themselves against dislocation. With central assistance limited to the most needy, the rest have incentives to use whatever parts of the national welfare system prove serviceable in the construction of local mechanisms for reducing the risks and costs of dislocation. We noted in passing in Chapter 2 that national agencies like FÁS and Forbairt were already taking an active role in helping firms adjust to new conditions of competition (and it is through that experience that they have gained an expert knowledge of industrial organisation in the Irish economy). The Area-Based Partnerships are contributing to the construction of a system of effective local adjustment precisely by helping to integrate efforts to improve the competitiveness of firms with efforts to increase the employability of residents in the local community. In this sense, the ABPs, together with decentralised economic development agencies, might, given the spare concertation at the centre, form the motor elements of a type of social partnership adapted to current conditions. Again, only time will tell. (This issue will be taken up again in Chapter 5.)

OTHER LOCAL DEVELOPMENT PARTNERSHIP PROGRAMMES

At the same time that actors on the domestic political scene were creating a new form of national partnership and contemplating decentralisation, programmes sponsored by individual government departments and by the European Union were using related ideas to achieve sectoral goals, notably in rural development and poverty programmes.

The Pilot Area Programme for Integrated Rural Development (IRD) and LEADER

One of the first such programmes was the Pilot Area Programme for Integrated Rural Development (IRD), which covered the years 1988 to 1990. It was organised by the Department of Agriculture to raise income levels in rural areas, principally by increasing employment opportunities. As the programme was modestly financed, however, its activities were largely confined to brokering relations between local development groups and individuals, on the one hand, and public and private providers of funds, on the other. Operations were confined to 12 independent pilot regions, each of which was assessed as forming a cohesive economic unit and had a maximum population of around 15 000. In each pilot area, a local co-ordinator was appointed and given the task of facilitating the local community's development efforts. The first task of the co-ordinator in each region was to organise a core group. This group consisted of representatives of voluntary organisations and normally had eight to ten members. The core group was, in effect, the body responsible for the operation of the programme in each area. In the beginning, most initiatives came from the co-ordinator, but the intention was that with time the core group would become the main initiator of programmes.

Founding principles of the programme were that groups should learn from each other and that no group should be left to develop in isolation from the others. To this end, both co-ordinators and core group members had to visit their counterparts at regular intervals and a good deal of the funding for the project was spent on activities involving more than one group.

Despite its modest scope and resources, the IRD arguably demonstrated the benefits of co-ordination on the local level, the potential utility of a local development agency in marshalling dispersed resources and the ability of local groups to find imaginative responses to local problems when given sufficient room to manœuvre. According to an evaluation of the programme, many of the 400 projects launched under its aegis involved significant local co-ordination of interests and funding, and, conversely, few would have been undertaken in the absence of some form of brokerage.[43]

The LEADER I initiative superseded the Pilot Area Programme for Integrated Rural Development and was both wider in coverage and more substantially funded.

This continent-wide EU programme, which grew out of an influential EU report on the future of rural society, was designed to identify innovative solutions to problems of economic stagnation, out-migration and underemployment in rural areas. In its first phase in Ireland, it provided for the establishment of 16 local development "companies", which operated between 1991 and 1994 with a total budget of around Ir£ 2-3 million each.

In practice, there was considerable continuity between the IRD and the subsequent LEADER programme, with the Department of Agriculture again acting as the responsible department. In this case, local actors were invited to form partnership companies, legal entities rather than loose groupings, and to bid for LEADER contracts. Because of their prior experience and organisation, several of the groups selected were those that had participated in the IRD programme. Others, however, antedated the IRD, having been formed on an independent basis unconnected with national programmes. Finally, some groups came together specifically for the programme, often with the idea of advancing some specific end, such as enterprise creation, rather than reactivating the wider community, which was often the motivation for more established groups.

"Partnership" is less precisely defined in the formal constitution of LEADER companies than in those of the Area-Based Partnerships. As with the latter, LEADER partnerships are constituted as legal limited-liability companies (or, in some cases, co-operative associations). But the size, composition, and organisational structure of their boards, as set out in the individual articles of association may, and do, vary greatly from one company to another. For example, while the average company board has about fourteen members, the largest have over twenty and the smallest five or six, as a result of local economic and institutional circumstances, not the extent of a company's geographical area. Board members represent community and voluntary groups, local sectoral interests such as farming groups and chambers of commerce and state agencies such as FÁS, Forbairt, SFADCO and Teagasc. Importantly, local government representatives are not excluded from participation. Unlike the Area-Based Partnerships, the balance of representation among the sectors is not determined by the constitution. The average board of 14 members contains five nominees from community groups, four from the private sector, two from the local authority and three from statutory bodies, but the distribution of groups varies from board to board. Because the representation of all interests in the community is not guaranteed, and given the importance, nonetheless, of representativeness to the company's operation, in some cases a community consultative council has been formed to broaden access to a LEADER company's decision-making process. Moreover, the decision-making process itself differs from company to company. In some areas, for instance, the management staff of the LEADER company assess individual projects and make funding decisions, with the board providing strategic direction. In others, Cavan/Monaghan for example, the directors are personally involved in assessing projects. The advantage of this flexibility is that boards can be shaped locally, thus reducing the feeling of having structures imposed from above. On the other hand, the boards so constructed may reflect the needs of local political comity more than operational considerations.

The programme's chief weaknesses, according to a recent evaluation (which was otherwise largely positive), were the closely related assumptions that working partnerships could be created almost overnight and that projects could be launched quickly and funded for brief periods.[44] In fact, the time needed to establish a board of directors and set up an office was typically longer than had been expected, which significantly reduced the time available for pursuing substantive goals before the pilot phase ended. Moreover, there was a significant delay before the staff in many LEADER companies felt competent to assess and respond to project applications. As a result, it was often only in the last half or even third of the programme's overall funding period that the LEADER companies were fully operational.

The success of the LEADER I programme has led to the inauguration of LEADER II, which involves expansion of the scheme to a much greater area (though without a proportionate increase in funding). The role of local development groups funded through the LEADER II programme is likely to be more developmental in the future, partly because other funding sources have been created through the EU's various Operational Programmes for 1994-99. LEADER I companies that have also qualified for funding under the successor LEADER II programme will have the significant advantages of prior experience and accumulated competence. This should enable LEADER II companies to target funding so as to complement rather than duplicate other sources, particularly in the area of enterprise creation where both the County Enterprise Boards (described below) and the Department of Agriculture can provide financial support. For example, the Cavan/Monaghan Rural Development Co-op Society Ltd., a LEADER I company, proposes to allocate 50 per cent of its LEADER II funding to training, animation and technical assistance, including the appointment of community development officers to liaise with community group organisers, and thus to raise the likelihood that the complementary resources will be well-used.

County Enterprise Boards

The County Enterprise Boards are the third major initiative. Here again, the current programme grew from a pilot project: a small-business grant support scheme that operated in ten counties in western Ireland. In the pilot areas, the forerunners of the County Enterprise Boards were concerned almost exclusively with project-by-project grant provision. Applications were assessed locally according to criteria established nationally. The programme was expanded to all counties in 1993, but funding remained limited until EC support was obtained through the Operational Programme for Local, Urban and Rural Development the following year.

The establishment of the national scheme in 1993 did not immediately change the focus of the initiative, which remained a system of small grants disbursed directly by the County Enterprise Boards (CEB) to individual entrepreneurs. However, the CEB remit has recently been expanded to include both the provision of a wider range of business support services and responsibility for the development of an enterprise development plan for their county.

The CEBs operate under the mantle of the Ministry of Enterprise and Employment as locally controlled companies, along the same general lines as the ABPs and LEADER companies. But within this similarity there are two substantial differences. First, the Department of Enterprise and Employment appears to exercise more control over the activities of the CEBs than the Department of Agriculture does the LEADER companies or, under different conditions, than ADM does the ABPs. Second, the board of directors of a CEB must include representatives of the local government, which is not the case for the Area-Based Response or LEADER partnership companies. Indeed, as if to underscore this connection with the established jurisdictions of government, the CEBs were often initially housed in local authority buildings and were staffed with personnel from the local government. From this perspective the CEBs are an attempt to attach the motor power of co-ordinated local initiatives to the machinery of both local government and national administration, while meshing each of the latter more tightly to the former.[45]

On paper, the responsibilities of the County Enterprise Boards, as described in the Operational Programme, are numerous and give the boards a strategic position in enterprise and job creation. The Operational Programme portrays the CEBs as a necessary complement to programmes of community empowerment with the crucial task of providing a "suitable top-down framework by which the Government and the EU can further facilitate co-operation between the State development agencies and local authorities on the one hand and the local community groups involved in enterprise development on the other."[46] However, until now the place of the CEBs within the wider institutional structure has remained unclear. The new "expansion" CEBs are still finalising their County Enterprise Plans and putting in place the mechanisms that will be necessary to implement them. Those with the benefit of an early start under the pilot programme, however, have been reluctant to go beyond the original emphasis on grant support to strategic planning and identification of support services other than financing.[47] The process of reviewing County Enterprise Plans is partly motivated by a desire on the part of the Department of Enterprise and Employment to coax the CEBs towards a more developmental role.

The New Situation: The Operational Programme for Local Urban and Rural Development, 1994-99

The successful implementation of this series of pilot programmes and the more general shifts in emphasis of the government's policy have greatly influenced the negotiation of the Operational Programme for Local Urban and Rural Development, 1994-99, co-funded by the European Commission and the Irish government. This is one of a number of EU-supported Operational Programmes, including both Agriculture and Tourism, that have been integrated into the Community Support Framework for Ireland which was agreed between the Irish government and the European Commission on the basis of the government's National Development Plan. The structures envisaged in this agreement were in turn endorsed by the social partners in the Programme for Competitiveness and Work, the successor agreement to the PNR and PESP.

The Operational Programme therefore marks the first formal efforts to integrate the rural and urban experiments in partnership that, as we have seen, grew up side by side, influenced each other in subtle ways, yet remained administratively distinct. The Programme puts local development aspects of the PESP in a wider local development framework which includes sub-programmes dealing with Local Enterprise Development (administered by the Department of Enterprise and Employment and consisting of the County Enterprise Board scheme), Urban and Village Renewal (administered by the Department of the Environment), and Integrated Development of Designated Disadvantaged and Other Areas (administered directly by Area Development Management, under the auspices of the Department of the Taoiseach and consisting mainly of the Area-Based Partnerships).

The inclusion of local development programmes within an operational programme framework for five years represents a strong endorsement by the government and the European Union of local development policies and their satisfaction with the pilot programme thus far. The Operational Programme has, in particular, been endorsed by a range of policy-making or otherwise influential bodies in Ireland. These include, notably, the social partners, initially through the CRC, the body originally formed to monitor the PNR. Employers' associations have gone so far as to establish an Enterprise Trust to make use of the possibilities provided by the Operational Programme to co-ordinate local business support for local economic development initiatives. Finally, the National Economic and Social Forum and NESC have also embraced the approach in recent reports.[48]

The Operational Programme offers two distinct advantages for the Area-Based Partnerships and the County Enterprise Boards. First, it provides more secure funding for a longer time. Funds for both projects are now guaranteed to 1999. Previously the partnerships had been dependent on three-year, national agreements subject to the vicissitudes of politics; the County Enterprise Boards had only interim funding. Second, the programme provides an opportunity to co-ordinate operations and more clearly define the roles and responsibilities of the various entities whose activities it supports.

The scope for co-ordination between the Area-Based Partnerships and the CEBs is highlighted in the text of the Operational Programme.

> Since County Enterprise Boards serve primarily as catalysts for enterprise creation and development, it will be entirely within their remit to delegate to Partnerships or other local communities, on an agency basis, responsibility for discharging particular enterprise support functions relative to their areas or sectors. The Partnerships will retain an important remit, as part of their integrated approach to local development, to support enterprise creation and development. Their target group will, however, be the unemployed, especially the long-term unemployed and persons who are otherwise socially excluded, differing from the generalised target group of the County Enterprise Boards. Accordingly, it is feasible for each structure to fulfil its remit concurrently by differentiation of target groups.[49]

As the instrument of this co-ordination, the Operational Programme specifies the creation of County Strategy Groups (CSGs). Their task is to integrate the activities of all the local development groups, both state-sponsored and voluntary, operating within a county area. The CSGs are composed of the chairs of the County Enterprise Boards, Area-Based Partnerships, LEADER companies and County Tourism Committees, along with the county manager (the unelected chief executive officer of each county).

The groups are even newer than the CEBs who count among their constituent institutions. They met for the first time in late 1995, and are currently preparing co-ordination strategies which aim to set out the functions and strengths of each development group, thereby avoiding duplication of and competition among local development efforts. Given their recent formation it is impossible to give even a preliminary indication of their prospects. So fluid is the situation that their formal structure is still under review. For example, the government, in response to questions about the accountability of the Strategy Groups, is currently proposing to alter their composition as set out in the Operational Programme to include elected local government representatives.

Political commitment to local development was reinforced by the appointment of a Minister for Local Development. The fact that the same Minister also has responsibility for European Affairs should ensure that Ireland's European policy is informed by the lessons of the local development approach at home.

CONCLUSION

The move towards consensus and partnership in policymaking thus began with two parallel movements that have begun to converge but have yet to find a stable meeting point. One of these original movements, growing out of the PNR and the PESP, reflected the deep concerns of domestic politics and addressed a range of economic issues, initially on a national basis, and then in local, particularly urban settings. The other, growing out of the Integrated Rural Development programme, LEADER I (along with other programmes not discussed here such as Poverty III) were inspired by EC priorities and used models developed in Brussels. These two movements have now begun to merge, to the point that most local development programmes are now partially funded under EU Operational Programmes.

But full merger or integration is still, plainly, a distant hope. The paradox of decentralisation from the centre manifests itself as institutional confusion. Acting on delegated authority from above, local programmes create projects that in turn cross and confuse boundaries between local jurisdictions and various levels of the national bureaucracies. Initiatives such as the CSGs, that aim to reintroduce order to the result may achieve their purpose, or add further clutter to the confusion. Partnership extends the possibilities of participation in economic and social reconstruction to wider and wider groups, but the place of elected officials becomes harder to define. The Operational Programme has heightened perplexity. In placing local development partnerships at the centre of a broad EU-funded strategy, the Operational Programme has drawn attention to the exclusion or limited involvement of local authorities in programmes that once seemed a hodge-podge of temporary measures. The initial omission of elected representatives in the design of the County Strategy Groups, for example, naturally provoked further concerns about the future accountability of economic development planning at county level. This and related questions will be addressed in Chapter 5.

All this, moreover, is not unique to Ireland. Throughout the EU, countries seem to be moving toward some form of public action that depends neither on the imaginary providence of a bureaucratic centre, nor on the fragile and potentially dispersive localism of community groups, but rather on a fusion of that which each of these does best.[50] To give substance to this possibility, and to see what virtues, if any, the new localism can demonstrate in practice, we turn next to an examination of the Area-Based Partnerships and, above all, to the projects by which they test their answers to the problems of economic stagnation and social exclusion.

4

PROJECTS AND PARTNERSHIPS:
TRANSFORMING THE LOCAL CONTEXT

INTRODUCTION

The very characteristics that allow the partnerships to be innovative also make them difficult to describe let alone evaluate systematically. They are, to begin with, amorphous. Although all are similarly constituted, and governed by similar rules, each is essentially a collection of varied and evolving projects. Put another way, the partnerships *are* the projects. They are animated by the projects they undertake; and as these change through the exploration of their tasks, the partnerships – what they do, how they conceive of their purpose and prospects – change perforce with them.

A rough first measure of the pace and direction of these changes is the gap between, on the one hand, the Action Plans presented by the local development groups at the onset of their operation as well as other expressions of their initial intent and, on the other, current reports on the work they have actually undertaken. For example, *Progress through Partnership*, the final evaluation of the pilot phase of the Area-Based Response found that the development of the initiative "has seen a shift in most areas away from a one-track approach to the reintegration of unemployed people into the labour market and towards a local development approach that incorporates enterprise, employment, training and education as well as community development, environmental and infrastructural issues as part of a package."[51] Many of these fields of activity, moreover, did not appear at all in the initial strategic plans, but were added later.

The comparison between expected and achieved results is even more striking. The final evaluation of the EU Global Grant, which brings together data from the original 12 partnerships and a number of other local development groups funded through the same grant, demonstrates that many more enterprises were assisted and unemployed people trained than had been projected. It was originally foreseen that up to 300 enterprises could be assisted and up to 400 people given business skills/entrepreneurship training. In fact, the numbers were 1 800 and 1 600 respectively. The most impressive figures are for training/education, including employability training, for the unemployed. Some 800 persons had been expected to participate in programmes and over 7 000 actually did, of whom over 80 per cent were unemployed.[52]

These panoramic studies alone, however, would shed little light on the programme's overall impact, nor on its potential and shortcomings. Firstly, they normally have neither the scope to report in detail just what assistance was given to firms and individuals, and how, nor to characterise the robustness of the outcomes they register. Do the persons placed in jobs keep them? Will the newly founded firms survive? More fundamentally, by listing activities and initial results, such studies cannot fully take into account the truly innovative and subtle aspects of the partnerships and of projects like Paksort – the way they change the meaning of activities such as job or firm creation and the environment in which these possibilities can be realised. The difficulty of describing quantitatively the work of the partnerships and deciding where credit should lie is suggested by one example. The partnerships' successes in getting unemployed people to set up new businesses depended significantly on their successful support of the introduction of an Area Allowance (Enterprise), or AA(E), which provides continuing benefit entitlements to people aiming at self-employment. Between 1993 and 1994, 321 people approached the Northside Partnership alone with business ideas; of those people almost one-third were eligible for AA(E) benefits. Statistics on persons placed could overlook such changes and can say little about what part of the increase in entrepreneurial activity was due directly to the partnership. They therefore distract attention from contributions that may be more enduring and pervasively effective than any single project.

A full treatment of the partnerships from this more comprehensive point of view would consider the evolution of each in its local setting, its relation to the others, and the influence of the partnerships as a whole on national institutions. Such a presentation is as far beyond our means as the evaluation of the projects by the standard methods of controlled experiment discussed in the first chapter. In place of an integrated and comprehensive account, we offer case studies of projects undertaken by the partnerships we visited, generally considered to be among the most active and successful. More precisely, we are reporting on what the best of the partnerships regard as the best of their projects. But if the aim of decentralisation is to allow the local protagonists to find new ways of doing things, where else should a review of the experiment start than with a careful, critical look at what those protagonists judge to be the best they have to show?

In presenting the case studies, we distinguish between groups operating in urban and rural areas. Urban partnerships focus on job placement, training for industrial employment and enterprise creation, both in manufacturing and services. They are also inevitably involved in tackling the social problems associated with disadvantaged urban areas. The rural partnerships, combating underemployment as much as unemployment, concentrate on projects that aim to knit the territory more tightly together, and counteract the dispersal of the population by providing services and infrastructural supports. It might seem, therefore, that despite the similarities of structure the two types of partnership are pursuing fundamentally different aims: "regeneration" in urban areas and "preservation" in rural areas. But we will see that in pursuing their respective ends, both are equally obliged to transform their settings; the similarity of the transformative methods they are inventing establishes a commonality beyond the outward differences.

LOCAL DEVELOPMENT PARTNERSHIPS IN AN URBAN SETTING

Changes in urban Ireland reflect the broad changes in urban life in advanced countries. New areas of relative affluence are appearing in many urban settings, while there is a general move out of inner city areas and a concentration of the poor in particular zones.

Of 35 areas designated as disadvantaged, 20 are urban, of which over two-thirds are located in Dublin. Their population as of the 1991 Census was 680 290, or 24 per cent of the total urban population. These localities are identified by high rates of early school leaving (<15); unemployment, particularly long-term unemployment; age dependency (the ratio below 14 years of age and above 65) and economic dependency (the ratio of the inactive to the active population); lone parent families; and numbers of residents in temporary housing. Conversely, educational levels and rates of labour force participation are low. According to these criteria, conditions within disadvantaged areas have declined not only absolutely, but with respect to the rest of the country over the past ten years. The gap between the poor and the others has widened, particularly with regard to the vulnerability to long-term unemployment.

The disadvantaged zones include both areas that have been home to the poor for generations, and newer developments typically defined by a peripheral location, the presence of public housing, and extremely high concentrations of unemployment. It is these latter areas that in public discussion in Ireland most graphically represent the inadequacies of past government economic and social policies.

The failure to co-ordinate economic and social policies can be illustrated by one example. The process of urbanisation in Ireland was rapid in the 1970s. Large housing estates were built on the outskirts of Dublin and other cities to house new migrants and ease the pressure on the congested city centres. The fate of these housing estates 20 years after their construction is common knowledge, and mirrors similar urban experiments in other European countries. Around the same period, Ireland went through a phase of rapid industrialisation, in great part through the attraction of foreign investment. This industrial expansion took place largely on specially-built industrial estates or on greenfield sites on the periphery of urban centres (though also in some more rural areas). By virtue of increased individual mobility and greater selectivity and competition in the labour market, the arrival of these industrial enterprises has affected a much larger labour market than would have been the case in the past.

The picture that emerges from much of the research, notably that of the Combat Poverty Agency and National Economic and Social Council, is one of a society becoming unacceptably fractured by socio-economic disparities, both in terms of individuals within the society and geographical areas in the country. The urban case examples below illustrate the situation in three of the most badly affected urban areas.[53]

The Tallaght Partnership

Tallaght is a suburb of Dublin constructed in the 1970s and early 1980s as part of a large-scale development plan for the Dublin region. The plan cleared inner-city slum housing and then relocated its residents, along with many persons migrating to Dublin from the rest of Ireland in this period, to purpose-built new towns on the periphery of the city. Rather than housing people in high-rise blocks, which by then were thought to lead to social decay, individual units with gardens were built on planned estates. Construction of this housing was the task of both private developers and the public authorities. Between 1971 and 1987, 16 000 new houses were built and the population of the town grew from 6 000 to nearly 70 000. Although some version of the original idea may have been workable, no entity was given responsibility for co-ordinating residential construction and the provision of complimentary services in the new town development. All communities in Tallaght suffered from the failure to match house building with essential infrastructural improvement. This failure was most acutely felt in the public housing estates on the perimeter of Tallaght. There the problems that plagued inner-city neighbourhoods in the 1960s re-emerged, compounded by the growing problems of long-term unemployment, and by distance from the centre. Although attempts are being made to develop a more complete infrastructure, including the placement of the largest shopping centre in Ireland in Tallaght, the area risks being caught in a cycle of deprivation and decline. The peripheral location of the area, the seemingly intractable problems of long-term unemployment, alongside a particularly young population (nearly 40 per cent of the residents were under 14 years of age in 1991) have contributed to Tallaght's reputation as an area balancing precariously between social and economic disaster and effective growth and development.

Local problems are so severe that an institution with resources as limited as those of the Tallaght Partnership cannot, and knows it cannot, hope to solve the problems of unemployment and marginalisation – certainly not by itself and not, in any case, immediately. The situation in Tallaght is too powerfully shaped by forces largely beyond local control for such a simple remedy.

Aware of the limitations imposed by their organisation's size and relative newness, staff and board members do not see their role in combating long-term unemployment as directly organising or running retraining or job placement programmes. The partnership, however, *can* question the use of funds in existing programmes, advocate and influence new directions, and run pilot programmes to ascertain whether particular ideas are viable or not.

The Tallaght Partnership accordingly sees itself primarily as a catalyst and facilitator,[54] drawing together relevant interests in projects that are intended to become components of an integrated response to development needs, nationally as well as locally. The Partnership's Youthstart Programme, for example, identified a gap in the guidance of young people from school to work. The national Youthreach programme offers a range of services to 15-17 year-olds after they leave school, including work experience, training and capacity building. Despite the broad scope of activities offered during the training period, the programme has had limited success in leading young people into stable employment afterwards. The main criticism of the programme is that it fails to equip participants with relevant work skills. On completion of the programme most choose between a low-wage, dead-end job and unemployment. FÁS and the local Vocational Education Committee (VEC) run a number of occupational and further training programmes that could link with Youthreach, but to qualify for most of them you must be over 21 years old. Most participants are 18 when they finish Youthreach and so would normally have to wait two years before being eligible for a next-step programme. During these two years they are at high risk of falling into a pattern of unstable employment leading to unemployment and then long-term unemployment. The Tallaght Partnership's Youthstart programme catches people as they leave the Youthreach programme and presents an alternative path that emphasises practical skills training over a period of two years. Drawing on this experience, the partnership is able to advise FÁS on the formulation of a more integrated, supportive policy for a particular vulnerable target group.

Just as the partnership calls on its local experience in urging reform on the higher authorities, so it calls on the experience of potential customers/users of new services in Tallaght by directly involving them in the design and delivery of the projects that affect them. For example, people with disabilities are centrally involved in the planning and implementation of the HORIZON (Disabled) programme, which aims to overcome the pigeonholing of the disabled in particular types of programmes. This programme depends upon close consultation between the rehabilitation and education service providers and the disabled in order to broaden the choices available to them. The guiding principle is that the disabled themselves should decide what kinds of services they need and in what context – rather than being taken automatically under the wing of a service for the disabled which immediately sets them apart. The service providers are being informed by their target group and learning to rethink their role.

In other areas the partnership acts more as a co-ordinator, with other community organisations and state agencies taking care of delivery. Its management of the Plato programme, and its decision to pass on supervision of that programme once its success was assured to the local Chamber of Commerce (and now the South Dublin County Enterprise Board) is a particularly clear illustration.

Plato

Plato, built on a model developed in Belgium, is a business training network. Local owner/managers are encouraged to learn from one another and from the advice of local large enterprises, who act as the facilitators of small working groups. At present, the Plato group at Tallaght consists of 60 small local companies and 10 larger "parent" firms. These latter include Asea Brown Boveri, Gallahers, Hallmark Cards, Hewlett Packard, Hoechst, Irish Biscuits, Johnson & Johnson, Loctite, Nestle Rowntree, Roadstone and RTC Tallaght, some of whom are recognised as leading practitioners of the new corporate decentralisation.

The objectives of the programme are to establish a broadly based business-to-business support structure which provides opportunities for SME owner/managers to develop their management skills and creates opportunities for commercial development through local and international networking. These activities both depend on and encourage interfirm co-operation.

The selection of appropriate participant companies is made by Plato staff, who conduct interviews with the owner/managers or managers of prospective members. Companies are judged on the basis of criteria such as the desire to expand, reach new markets, or commercialise new products. At bottom, ambition to expand, perhaps by serving foreign markets, is the main condition for participation. The programme is thus aimed, in Tallaght, at the emerging sector of indigenous industry described in the last part of Chapter 2 – those companies that are moving beyond domestic markets by selling either directly abroad or to firms that do, and anxious to incorporate new technologies and production techniques in adapting to an open economy. Those selected for participation are grouped with companies of similar dimensions or sectors to ensure as far as possible that the issues raised in the groups are of general interest.

The concerns of the groups have changed during the two years of their existence in ways that reflect the growing importance of projects concerned with the adoption of the new production methods. At the beginning, as is normally the case in such situations, the participants were absorbed in learning to talk to other business people openly, in exchanging ideas, and in realising that their own, apparently unique problems were actually shared by many in the group (and may have been solved by still others). Group projects and discussion focused on basic themes such as industrial relations and time management. More recently, however, projects have begun to focus on ISO 9 000 certification, quality control, and the like. About half the leaders chosen from large firms to guide the groups are specialists in quality control, logistics, production management, or industrial engineering – the core disciplines of the new organisational model.

Plato itself cannot provide training in ISO 9 000 or related areas, but the partnership provides a framework in which training services tailored to particular needs of member firms can be obtained through the statutory training bodies. Firms from Plato groups, by training together, can purchase the consulting services they need from public or private providers on better terms.

A recent independent survey of the programme's participants showed – as surveys of select groups of dynamic firms often do – that almost all were satisfied with their experience of the network. More revealing, a large majority credited participation with improvements in operations, marketing and financial management. The average increase in turnover of the companies involved was 19 per cent and 24 per cent growth in employment (93 new jobs created).

Box.   **Expanding the Plato model**

The Plato model described above presents a good example of a successful programme is being "mainstreamed".

In theory, the Plato model is portable because it is, at heart, a general method for transferring knowledge from those with more experience of a particular environment to those with less. The particular institutions for transferring the knowledge will vary according to the environment and the know-how appropriate to it.

But this means that, in practice, the model can only work if the actors can accurately judge who can teach and who can learn what from whom. The idea that little firms can grow by listening to big ones is simply too vague to identify the interlocutors and themes that will sustain continuing exchange. In the Plato programme as run by Tallaght Partnership, the groups are composed of small businessmen who aim to grow established companies, often through expansion into foreign markets; their mentors are managers of local large enterprises that have a good grip on the new disciplines needed for international competition, and are familiar with many dynamic, local small firms, from whom they purchase components or services. This pattern cannot be easily transposed to, for example, Dundalk (whose partnership is discussed below), where there are few advanced large firms, and growing, established small businesses are scarce. So in implementing the Plato model (as

(continued on next page)

(continued)

part of a cross-border initiative with the Newry and Mourne Enterprise Agency in Northern Ireland and the Louth County Enterprise Board) the Dundalk Partnership is adapting it. The project groups will be comprised of new entrepreneurs mentored by managers of existing small businesses within an enterprise centre that the partnership is establishing.

The South Kerry Partnership (see below) is also considering introducing the scheme, again adapting it to local circumstances. Kerry is one of the more remote and rural regions of the country, with little industry and an economy supported by tourism and agriculture. There are few small manufacturing companies in South Kerry and almost no large enterprises. But it may be that start-ups in complementary activities can "mentor" each other, or organise joint study tours to review best practices elsewhere in Ireland or abroad.

The potential risks of confusing form and substance are suggested by the results of a recent feasibility study conducted by the Department of Enterprise and Employment to assess whether the Plato model could be taken on by the County Enterprise Boards. The report details the criteria necessary for a solid Plato network (for example, an SME base of 500 suitable companies of whom 80-100 are potential participants in the programme, at least ten large companies each with over 20 managers willing to participate, and a suitably compact geographical area). The report concluded that the CEBs were ideally suited as host organisations and provided the best available opportunity to meet the local management requirements for the introduction of new Plato networks in new areas of the country. In line with the criteria specified, County Enterprise Boards have spearheaded the implementation of Plato programmes in five areas – the greater Cork and greater Limerick areas, Louth (allied with Newry in Northern Ireland), Kildare and South Dublin (an expansion of the original Tallaght project).[55]

But the central methodological question remains whether to find areas that suit the Plato "model" of large-firm mentoring, or find ways of reinterpreting mentoring to meet the needs of the economic activity in various settings.

Exactly how the parent companies, who initially saw their participation as a public service, now see the possibilities of the situation is hard to say. Several parent companies noted, for example, the beneficial effect acting as group leader had on their own executives. The choice of group leaders from production-related specialities will have alerted them, if their own contact with local suppliers had not done so before, that the small firms amidst them are beginning to modernise. In time, acting on the first-hand knowledge of their own managers, they may well begin to purchase products or services from the more capable participants, and this would itself recommend participation to further circles of small firms, and so on.

The Northside Partnership

The Northside Partnership covers the area from Coolock to Kilbarrack (known as Dublin's Northside), a relatively new suburb of Dublin built, like Tallaght, in the 1970s. The area is considered to be one of the worst unemployment blackspots in the country. The current rate of unemployment in the Northside Partnership area is 31 per cent. For people between the ages of 15 and 21, the rate is over 35 per cent. Thirty-four per cent of the inhabitants of the area left school before the age of 15 and a further 19 per cent did so at the age of 15. For a substantial number of those living within the area, neither the educational context provided by their families, their communities, or their own experiences within the formal school system adequately prepare them to enter the labour market.

For the Northside Partnership, the central problem in the local labour market is that local residents are not being hired by firms on the industrial estates in the area. Among the firms located nearby are several successful and relatively large foreign and domestic companies. The housing estates' notoriety for high rates of long-term unemployment and various social problems may make residents unappealing to recruiters. A main aim of the Partnership is therefore to find strategies to overcome what seems to be a reluctance to hire the local long-term unemployed. One of the principal means to this end has been the creation of a local firm, Speedpak, whose purpose is to hire and train the unemployed, particularly the most disadvantaged, and demonstrate both through their success in operating a commercially viable plant and in obtaining jobs elsewhere afterwards that the community from which they come has a place in the active economy.

Speedpak

Speedpak's main activity is short-run, contract packaging and subassembly. To date, its operations have included subassembly of toys and other products and shrink-wrapping of promotional materials used in advertising campaigns: toothbrushes, for example, will be attached to boxes containing tubes of a popular toothpaste, and the combination is then offered to the public for several months in the hope that the popularity of the latter will increase sales of the former. Production runs of promotional items or seasonal gifts are typically too short to be of interest to large domestic packagers, so Speedpak can offer domestic customers the advantage of quick turnaround in a market where advertising and seasonal deadlines traditionally made recourse to foreign firms risky. Speedpak currently employs 30 people and the firm is so successful in placing its employees in other jobs that it can recruit around 30 new staff every six months.

This choice of line of business and market were determined by the firm's goal of teaching the unemployed, including many with little work experience at all, a skill that would increase their chances of long-term employability, and doing so under conditions as demanding as those they would find in any well organised company. The Economic Committee of the Northside Board thus began by selecting a consultant to ascertain which skill or skills now contribute to employability. This consultant, a former production manager at a Cadbury's confectionery plant, in turn conducted a thorough if informal survey of about one hundred of his former colleagues and associates. His interlocutors, he found, were nearly unanimous in holding that craft skills by themselves were no longer highly valued. Instead, the ability to solve problems in groups – the ability, that is, to work with others in detecting and resolving problems in work set-up or organisation – was seen as sufficient for many of the new jobs and a necessary precondition for learning the more specific technical skills required in others. Given the limits of the start-up capital that could be provided by the Northside Partnership, the best way to design a firm that regularly "produced" the kinds of problems teams would need to solve was to use simple technology that constantly had to be reconfigured to meet new demands on a tight schedule. Shrink-wrapping items for time-sensitive markets provided the right combination of technical simplicity and organisational rigor, while meeting the additional criterion of potential commercial viability as well.

To check whether Speedpak actually teaches the lesson of team problem-solving it advertises, we applied the test, suggested in Chapter 1, of taking the firm at its word, and asked a group of four employees (the youngest in his late teens, the oldest in her early forties) to show us the most recent problem they had solved. The week before, they said, a customer had overestimated the number of shrink-wrapped units – a box of detergent joined to a small bar of soap – that could fit in the cartons supplied: the customer had calculated four units, stacked on their broad side, per carton, but only three would fit. With only three units per carton there was so much empty space that the contents shifted in a way that could have caused damage, and the supply of cartons was insufficient, at that ratio, to pack the whole order. As a solution the workgroup proposed rotating the units and packing them in two layers of two each, end to end. To the evident satisfaction of the Speedpak employees, the customer's packing department admitted its error, approved the change, and the job proceeded. If problem solving in groups is the foundation of employability, these employees are likely to find jobs easily.

While Speedpak is intended to survive without operating subsidies, it is unclear whether it can, or, indeed, how its operating expenses should be calculated. For one thing, the wages it effectively pays depend in part on the social welfare benefits available under various programmes to its employees. Disputes regarding eligibility for these benefits has periodically put Speedpak (and the Northside Partnership) at odds with the statutory agencies. For another, wage levels aside, the firm's costs are increased by the need to constantly "graduate" the most advanced employees into jobs in other companies and recruit inexperienced replacements who often must initially wrestle with social problems that effect their motivation.

The deeper question, of course, is whether Speedpak is best judged as a firm or as a new kind of vocational school, and if the latter, then how commercial discipline can be maintained without imposing impossible budgetary constraints on the organisation. We will see in Chapter 5 that neither this question, nor, for that matter, any like it, is being systematically discussed either by those monitoring the developments in the partnerships or by other partnerships pursuing strikingly similar projects.

The absence of this discussion is all the more disquieting because the success of Speedpak, if it does indeed prove sustainable, would have consequences far beyond the number of persons the firm itself directly trains and places. Leaving aside its possible influence on the reorganisation of vocational training, the firm could have a substantial influence locally by changing employers' perceptions of the capacities and prospects of the unemployed. To see why such a change is important, and how, beyond the demonstration provided by Speedpak, it might be realised, we consider a complementary programme of the Northside Partnership, Contact Point, that focuses more on placement than training.

Contact Point

Almost two-thirds of vacancies in local companies are not advertised. In many settings this would not disadvantage local job seekers, as information about openings is circulated by word of mouth, and employees who live close to their work simply spread the news to their local circles. But many employees of Northside firms live outside the area, so word of mouth actually disadvantages those who do. Piled on top of the stereotype of the housing estate resident as unsuited for work, word of mouth advertisement walls off local jobs from those closest to them. The Contact Point programme run by the Northside Partnership is intended to foster a close link between local recruiters and the local unemployed in order to overcome this barrier.

The programme, based on a Dutch model, looks to both the supply and the demand sides of the labour market. While many labour market programmes provide individual counselling to the unemployed as they search for jobs, few effectively combine this with building close links with potential employers. To do this, Contact Point offers employers a register of all *local* job seekers, with the assurance that each has been interviewed and counselled by Contact Point staff. The programme also provides employers with advice on framing job specifications, screening of suitable applicants, and identification of possible additional training needs after placement.

The relation between Contact Point and the leading local employers began informally. At the start of the programme, members of the Northside Partnership board, who are themselves businessmen or managers, held breakfast meetings with other local employers to introduce and refine the idea of using the partnership as a recruitment instrument. The partnership offers to identify local people for job openings and, where necessary, provide training and retraining for those who need it before taking on a particular position. Regular consultations are now held between Contact Point "mediators", who are usually from an industry background, and employers to define immediate or upcoming recruitment needs. Appropriate local applicants are then identified from an up-to-date register of local job seekers which is compiled on the basis of personal interviews carried out between the same mediators who liaise with local employers and the unemployed person. These interviews could result in a period of training or retraining before the job search process begins; in others, the mediator concludes that the person has the capabilities that local employers are looking for. In each case, the mediator can base the assessment on an intimate knowledge of the recruitment needs of local employers in terms of skills, experience and motivation.

Thus, through Contact Point, the partnership, in effect, guarantees or sponsors local people and, through projects such as Speedpak and the guidance programme known as "Individual Career Path Counselling", ensures that they are equipped with the necessary basic work skills for the particular job.

The success of the programme's integrated approach was recognised in the Interim Report of the Task Force on Long-Term Unemployment which, in July 1995, recommended the implementation of a nation-wide Local Employment Service based around the Contact Point model.[56] Among other things, the report identified a lack of high quality guidance and counselling services for the unemployed, which meant that some of the positive outcomes from training and educational programmes were going to waste and that job matching was somewhat haphazard. Contact Point's Individual Career Path Counselling was selected as the practical model for the development of local advisory services that emphasise personal guidance and accompaniment of the unemployed combined with a much closer link between the employment services and local enterprises than was possible in the past.

Dundalk Employment Partnership

Dundalk is a border town. For a variety of reasons, some linked to the troubles in nearby Northern Ireland, the quality of life of many residents has deteriorated over the past decade. Before the troubles and the onset of industrial restructuring the town had a fairly strong manufacturing base. Several branch plants of British companies in the footwear and clothing industries were located there along with major Irish firms. The decline in both Irish and British manufacturing throughout the 1980s, combined with an unattractive location along a closed border, led to a substantial reduction in manufacturing jobs in the town, and so to large-scale unemployment.

Dundalk is currently classed as one of the six most deprived areas in Ireland. At 28.4 per cent, the level of unemployment is half again as high the national average. Forty-five per cent of the unemployed are older than 34, and there has been a vertiginous increase in the number of long-term unemployed within that age group. For example, between 1991 and 1995, while the overall level of unemployment remained the same, the number unemployed for more than two years increased by over 40 per cent; the number on the Live Register for more than three years rose by 50 per cent. The rate of long-term unemployment is particularly high on local authority housing estates which, as elsewhere, increasingly are home to second and third generation unemployed. In Dundalk the share of the housing stock rented by the Local Authority, the share of semi-skilled or unskilled manual workers in the workforce, and the share of households where the head of household may never have been in paid employment are all above the respective national averages. The area has a very high level of early school leaving and, with a reduced job base, employers often insist on formal qualifications even for the lowest skill jobs.

Forbairt and the IDA have succeeded in attracting some inward investment into the area, and this has helped stabilise the rate of short-term unemployment during the past two years. But the arrival of industries from outside the area has had little effect on the rate of long-term unemployment, which has continued to rise dramatically. As in Tallaght, those who have not recently had a job are not likely to be considered for new ones.

The aim of the Dundalk Employment Partnership is therefore to improve the employability of the long-term unemployed by showing employers, and often the unemployed themselves, that those at the margins of or even outside the labour market can work to appropriate standards. The partnership's programmes increasingly revolve around developing enterprises that employ the long-term unemployed and encouraging the long-term unemployed to start their own businesses. Essentially, the partnership aims to work to change the perception of the long-term unemployed; from being the questionable part of a social question that sets them aside from others, to being another and fully legitimate component of the economic development process in which the town is engaged. An example is Paksort.

Paksort

Paksort is an enterprise established by the partnership in close collaboration with the Guinness Company, whose local brewery and packaging plant are both major employers in the town. Whereas the Speedpak project, whatever its formal budgetary constraints, is mainly concerned with, as it were, "commercialising" individuals by training them for employment elsewhere, Paksort has been designed as a commercial enterprise that will employ increasing numbers of permanent staff from the ranks of the long-term unemployed as it grows. It is meant to be, therefore, at least as much, if not more, a source of employment than a training ground for employability.

This difference aside, Paksort resembles Speedpak in fundamental ways. It, too, has identified a market opportunity in the increasing recourse or preference of large and medium-sized companies to decentralise production by sub-contracting processes that either need specialist equipment or that are based on short production runs.

In this case, the Guinness Packaging Plant, which had changed its entire returnable bottle stock to 33 cl. size, required an off-site bottle sorting plant to separate the different brand types according to colour or shape. The partnership was one of a number of potential contractors invited to tender for the work. Close contact between the partnership and high managers in the Guinness Company helped provide assurance that the partnership's winning tender was indeed credible.

After securing the contract, the Dundalk Partnership recruited a manager with wide experience in the field, and then worked with the Guinness Packaging Plant to design the production line, define the requisite, and demanding, quality standards, and get the operation up and running.

Paksort works according to tight production and delivery schedules. Lorries unload cartons of bottles collected by wholesalers from their regional clients. These are then sorted and passed to the bottling plant for reuse. Stocks of sorted bottles at the packaging plant are kept to a bare minimum. Sorting errors would cause extremely costly disruption of the customer's high-speed bottling lines.

Participants in the programme are intended to get training in all phases of the process, with the ultimate aim being to develop proof they can work in a team to extremely high quality standards in a job demanding enormous concentration. As of our visit, however, quality control was is in the hands of a distinct group of inspectors, as in a traditional mass-production plant. It was unclear when, if ever, employees would participate in design of work organisation or, indeed, what responsibilities, beyond quality control, would eventually be assigned to the work "teams".

Paksort is an independent company, with its own board drawn from members of the partnership board. The Board of Paksort was designed such that the representatives brought to the board a range of practical financial, production/operations, and human resource expertise. The partnership's secretariat and outside business advisor complement the resources available through the board.

Paksort and the partnership are thus mutually defining. First and foremost, the partnership board was constructed such that the major local enterprise was intimately connected to the organisation's work, and could therefore indicate a potential enterprise opportunity of which community groups outside the formal partnership structure might not have been made aware. Second, the participation of the private enterprise gave the partnership's quasi-social enterprise a strong commercial orientation and forced the managers to adopt the same practices and standards as any other firm supplying the sponsoring company.

But all this intimacy comes at a price. Paksort's idea of teamwork comes from Guinness, not, as in the case of Speedpak, from its own canvass of best-practice. Paksort's freedom to experiment, moreover, is sharply limited by the need to meet its customer's extremely demanding production requirements. Finally, intimacy can often provoke suspicion of conspiracy. One of many long-term ways to allay such fears, and regain space in which to experiment that might be used to extend training and teamwork, would be to diversify production to serve other customers. That would both demonstrate Paksort's independence and force the firm to test its organisation in new and demanding settings.

This close counselling and guidance of enterprises and individuals is evident as well in the case of other enterprises started with the partnership's support. One of these is Eros Ltd. which grew out of the closure of a branch plant in Dundalk, a clothing unit of the British firm, Courtaulds. After the closure, the Dundalk Partnership helped one of the former managers to reorganise the plant as a stand-alone company. The starting point for the new enterprise was the realisation that the factory's workforce was highly skilled in the cutting and sewing of lycra and other materials used in swimwear and lingerie. With this pool of expert machinists, the enterprise can produce short batches of quality garments in various fabrics to customer specifications – precisely what is needed in lines of business like fashion swimwear where product lifespans are short and turnaround times are rapid even in comparison to other segments of the fashion industry.

The partnership provided business support to Eros Ltd., including a consultant to help prepare a business plan, assistance with an application to Forbairt (then IDA), plus secretarial and office services. Rather than offering financial help, which eventually came from government sources such as the IDA, the partnership mainly offered "hand-holding" and encouragement. The enterprise is now exporting to the UK and includes international mail order catalogues among its clients.

The partnership has provided similar services, on a smaller scale, to numerous unemployed persons looking to start businesses as diverse as barber shops, flower shops and music tutoring services. An important instrument used by the partnership to encourage these efforts is the Area Allowance for Enterprise (AA(E)), a programme that was developed by the partnerships and operates only where they do. Through this programme, potential entrepreneurs can retain full unemployment benefit for one year while they are starting a business, followed by 75 per cent the second year, 50 per cent the third, and so on. This entitlement is significantly higher than those offered through the "Back to Work" scheme, which starts at 75 per cent for the first year. It is the partnership rather than the Department of Social Welfare that determines eligibility. This allows for local co-ordination. Dundalk can support only so many attempts to start new barber shops simultaneously. And, of course, those projects that are approved can receive, right from the start, the kind of support they will need from a local institution familiar with their plans, confident in their abilities, and well-placed to find nearby solutions to problems. The development of a business plan, mentoring, the evaluation of progress, and consideration of eventual financial support are all connected from the first. In effect, the Dundalk Partnership, at its best, becomes in this way a kind of popular venture capitalist, nurturing new firms by providing both hands-on management support and "equity" financing on condition that the start-ups develop credible plans and meet their goals.

People Against Unemployment in Limerick (PAUL) Partnership

The PAUL Partnership was established as part of the EU Poverty III pilot programme. Although the parameters for defining poverty and the range of possible responses were broad in the Poverty III programme, in effect the PAUL Partnership, as its name suggests, viewed unemployment as the overriding concern.

In its initial phase, the partnership targeted four specific geographic areas, chosen on the basis of unemployment rate, rather than focusing on vulnerable groups. With the incorporation of the PAUL Partnership into the Area-Based Response to Long-Term Unemployment, the target area had to be widened beyond the four chosen areas to cover the entire city of Limerick. This expansion was opposed by some within the partnership, who would have preferred, if anything, narrowing rather than broadening the target area. Their fear was that expansion would jeopardise the inchoate forms of participative goal-setting and management that made the organisation's work effective. Inclusion of the partnership in the Area-Based Response, on the other hand, had the clear advantages of providing more secure and longer-term funding, and offering the opportunity to participate in a nationally co-ordinated response to long-term unemployment. We are simply in no position to say whether the costs of amalgamation have outweighed the benefits. But it is important to note that the partnerships are today, if anything, more threatened by disruption through expansion of the programme than ever before; and we will return to the problem below.

The PAUL Partnership, in any event, has been particularly successful in the area of welfare rights and advocacy on behalf of the unemployed. In particular, the partnership has been involved in successful "take-up" campaigns and other welfare information activities. Moreover, it has communicated the information collected through these activities to central government, with the result that it has had a sizeable influence on new legislation.

One example is the contribution of PAUL, together with other local development groups, to the transformation of the Social Employment Scheme into the Community Employment Scheme. The Social Employment Scheme (SES) was the government's main response to long-term unemployment at the time. The SES provided temporary part-time unemployment benefits to persons aged over 25 who had been out of work for more than one year. The income received by participants was broadly similar to that payable under the normal unemployment benefit programme. The SES was funded by the state training agency, FÁS, and implemented by local sponsors, often non-profit groups, public bodies, or local authorities. An evaluation of the programme in the Limerick area by the PAUL Partnership detected important flaws. For one thing, although participants earned slightly more money on SES than when drawing unemployment benefits, they lost their secondary benefits, of which the most important was the indispensable medical insurance card. For another, a number of schemes included no training component, even though this was supposed to be an integral part of the programme's approach, and participants rarely got the chance to use their existing skills. The results under the then-current legislation, moreover, were discouraging. The placement rate in long-term employment after completion of the programme was as low as 20 per cent. In 1992, SES in the twelve area partnerships was replaced by the Community Employment Development Programme (CEDP) again funded by FÁS, which provided enhanced training and retention of secondary benefits for the duration of the programme, as had been urged by PAUL and other local development groups.[57]

A second example of the partnership's use of local experience to guide reformation of national legislation concerns consumer credit. Working closely with the Mid-Western Health Board, PAUL founded the Money Advice Project, which provides low-income families with information, advice and support in managing their debts, and helps organise the supply of low-cost credit to residents of poor areas. The partnership's community-based advising services also provide access to special credit union accounts for participants. In addition, volunteers from the credit union offer workshops on money management (which 600 people attended last year), individual savings schemes have been established in conjunction with government employment programmes such as the Community Employment Programme, and a Young Person's Guide to Money has been produced. This project directly influenced the elaboration of the Consumer Credit Bill, and has been embraced by the Department of Social Welfare as part of its national Money Advice Programme.

Like the Tallaght Partnership, PAUL has come to focus increasingly on piloting innovative programmes. For example, between 1992 and 1994, PAUL ran a programme for single parents funded through the HORIZON element of the Human Resources Initiative which was one of the first programmes designed to integrate single mothers into the labour market. In so doing, it highlighted a number of factors that prejudice against their entering the workforce. Segments of the training have now been mainstreamed by the Limerick City Vocational Education Committee (VEC) and FÁS, and measures to favour lone parents have been introduced as a result. Similarly, the partnership formed a project to respond to a need among older people – particularly women with school-age children – who left school as early as 14 and now lack basic educational skills; and this project too is being mainstreamed by the VEC.

This list, which could be lengthened, is already long enough to suggest the danger of "dispersion". In pursuing many projects aimed at correction of existing programmes, PAUL may be trading immediate but limited benefits for the possibility of larger reforms through exploration of new ways of linking previously distinct services by combining, to take a speculative example, tenant participation in estate management with training in the management of personal debt or job preparation. Again, we are in no position to weigh costs and benefits, and one of the advantages of the system of democratic experimentalism we will discuss below is to allow systematic evaluation of the potential complementarities and conflicts between PAUL's emphasis on legislative reform and other strategies of innovation.

LOCAL DEVELOPMENT GROUPS IN RURAL AREAS

Rural areas throughout the OECD area have been severely affected by structural change over the past three decades. The process of adjustment in the rural economy is well-known. Technological advances, such as the development of high-yield crops, increase supply beyond stable demand, which results in downward pressure on prices. The more efficient producers continue to invest in new methods of cutting unit costs. Less efficient producers are forced to follow suit to maintain their market position relative to the leading producers. Those unable to maintain the necessary level of investment fail and are absorbed into larger farms. The land consolidation thus is, perhaps, the defining manifestation of restructuring, and one of the primary methods of reducing unit production costs. The process of agricultural restructuring is therefore characterised by increasingly large land holdings, a decline in the number of landholders, market dominance by capital-intensive, high-yield, large-acreage commercial farms and a movement out of agriculture or into non-traditional agricultural activities on the part of the smaller farmers.

The transformation of rural areas in Ireland generally parallels that of rural areas across Europe. The largest one-fifth of farms comprises almost two-fifths of all land and produces over two-thirds of all agricultural output. There are, however, important differences between the Irish context and that of other countries, and these differences are relevant here.

In Ireland, aggregation of landholdings did not take place on the same scale as elsewhere. The decline in individual agricultural incomes was certainly significant; neither a pastoral heritage nor political support from Dublin and Brussels could stave off the consequences of changing global trade patterns and pricing systems. Yet the effect of the decline in or increasing volatility of agricultural incomes has not so far had the effect on the shape of the rural landscape as in other countries.[58] While conventional agricultural employment in Ireland has shrunk, from 255 000 in 1973 to 144 000 in 1993, landholding has remained quite stable and land consolidation has been low.

The survival strategies of small Irish farmers in the face of agricultural restructuring include enhanced full-time farming on larger consolidated holdings; off-farm employment, combined with "after-hours" farming; and diversification into other, non-traditional activities. The breakdown among landholders is 40 per cent full-time farmers, 30 per cent part-time farmers drawing only a minority of their total household income from farming, and 30 per cent "after-hours" farmers. The number of persons in this last category increased by over 70 per cent between 1960 and 1987. Of all households whose head of household is classified as a farmer, the proportion of total household income deriving from agriculture has declined from 70 per cent in 1973 to 54 per cent in 1987.[59] Among those who have off-farm employment, studies show that a substantial group have "at least moderate levels of education" and "only a minority are engaged in unskilled manual work." On the other hand, small-scale farmers who stay in full-time farming either because they prefer it, are unqualified for other work, or are too geographically remote, are "among the most poverty prone groupings in Irish society."[60] The proportion of farmers with secondary incomes that exceed agricultural income increases, logically, as the holdings get smaller and also with proximity to urban centres. There are signs, however, that the pace of land consolidation and movement out of agriculture is increasing, largely because of reform of the Common Agricultural Policy CAP – before adequate diversification of the rural economy has taken place.

The reform of the CAP from support for market prices to direct income support in 1992 marks a significant shift with as yet uncertain implications. This reform tightens supply controls, significantly reduces production subsidies such as support prices, promotes agricultural restructuring through agri-environmental and forestry programmes and encourages early retirement of older farmers. The emphasis of the original CAP on intervention support within their traditional sphere of agriculture has now been replaced by a vaguer encouragement of alternative activities. For Ireland, at least in the view of the NESC, the programmes to promote diversification, while important, will not "compensate for the constraints imposed on conventional farming."[61]

The strength of Irish agriculture lies in its large dairy and meat co-operatives, who are increasingly sophisticated food processors. These co-ops, some of which are now public limited companies, include many thousands of small farmers and can provide a fairly stable market for milk or beef. This connection to world markets helps keep Irish agriculture in these sectors competitive; but it also increases the potential volatility of farm incomes by concentrating agricultural activities in areas dependent on politically set quota levels. In periods of quota reduction, moreover, the resources available for small producers to invest in production improvements, buy out surplus quota rights from less efficient producers, or start up new agricultural or non-agricultural activities is limited. These limitations explain, in part, why increasing demand for speciality food products in Ireland has largely been filled by imports into the country or by up-stream processing efforts by large indigenous agricultural enterprises, but not so much by small producers. The co-operative system has worked so well, it could be argued, that there is a lack of skills and experiences in other rural activities. This contrasts with other small OECD countries such as Belgium, where a large range of speciality products and foodstuffs have been developed and where small producers have formed small- or medium-sized co-operatives that engage in product and market research, but that nonetheless allow small farmers themselves to have hands-on experience of the process of developing new products, markets and technologies.[62]

A further, crucial complication is that strain in the agricultural sector is unlikely to be relieved, as it often was in the recent past, by the development of industry in the countryside. The option of off-farm employment in Ireland was encouraged initially by the spread of infrastructural services to rural areas. A significant proportion of rural dwellers with non-agricultural employment work for the public utility companies such as gas, electricity and water. In addition, for a period, the government adopted a policy of rural or regional industrialisation which involved the compilation of a list of 200 small rural settlements that were targeted as potential industrial sites. This policy rested largely on the attraction of foreign companies into areas previously without much industry, chiefly through the use of grant aid and other benefits. Its success, due to a combination of strong incentive packages and a preference among the locating companies for non-urban "greenfield sites", had a significant impact on rural areas. Thanks to these fast-growing export-oriented enterprises, the rural areas concerned experienced rates of industrial growth above those of the Dublin area throughout the 1970s. While in the Dublin area many traditional Irish firms producing internationally-traded goods such as textiles and footwear were being closed or restructured, firms locating in rural areas were in that period both protected by subsidies and largely concentrated in expanding industries. The arrival of foreign enterprises served to spread industrial production more evenly across the country than had been the case before.

The political prominence of regional industrialisation as a policy was affected by the classification of Dublin as an area of disadvantage, and thus a target for industrial redevelopment. This change, together with the reduction in the number of companies locating in Ireland, for reasons discussed in Chapter 2, have increased the competition for inward investment among Ireland's rural regions, all of which are agreed that Dublin still has major political and infrastructural advantages in the contest for new firms. Moreover, competition from other peripheral regions in Europe for "nomadic" branch plants has raised the stakes to the point that the incentives that need to be offered are enormously high and call into question the economic logic of the policy. The relocation of the Digital plant from Galway to Ayrshire in Scotland was a sobering example in this regard.

The upshot is that, though agriculture remains crucial, rural Ireland can no longer rely either on its long-standing strengths in the production of agricultural commodities or on rural industrialisation to undergird the vitality of areas that have lived off the land for generations. Indeed, economic development is no longer solely, or even primarily, a question of agricultural policy. It is now clear that the balanced development of rural areas depends on a range of factors such as: investment and industrial strategies, employment policies, education, health and other social services, housing and transportation facilities. With agricultural potential now no longer defining the potential for economic development, the advantages of a region must be viewed from this more comprehensive perspective. In Ireland, as in the rest of the OECD, all this has enhanced the prominence of strategic or integrative approaches to rural development.

From the vantage point of this integrative approach, the chief goal is to stabilise the population base and end dependence on out-migration. For most groups, the key to retaining a stable population base involves mastering three issues: 1) the provision of sufficient economic opportunities, which in the present day depends on the ability to supplement traditional agricultural activities with other income-generating activities; 2) the provision of adequate infrastructural and other services, ranging from transportation to education and training, and 3) the maintenance of a strong sense of community and promotion of community social and cultural support structures.

As a result of out-migration, unemployment in most rural areas is relatively low, compared with disadvantaged urban areas; but, as a result of the cumulative structural changes, underemployment is widespread. In contrast to partnerships in the urban areas, therefore, rural local development initiatives in rural areas do not generally have to become as involved in programmes to support and train the long-term unemployed. The emphasis in these areas can be, instead, on the creation of new and innovative farm enterprises, and on enhancing "marginal" employment – for example, supplementary off-farm activities, food processing of farm produce, rural tourism and so on.

The establishment of the Operational Programmes for Agriculture and Tourism, along with the expansion of the CEBs, means that funding is now available from other sources for projects that could be eligible for LEADER funding. For example, alternative farm enterprises such as deer farming and sport horse breeding were encouraged and assisted under the LEADER I programme but now they would be more likely to obtain funding through the Operational Programme for Agriculture. In theory, this gives greater scope for LEADER II to direct funds towards the more developmental or innovative projects, including animation of community develop- ment activities and provision of training programmes that lie outside the remit of the Operational Programmes and the CEB. For the same reasons, the various Operational Programmes should have the effect of freeing some resources that have been previously used for enterprise creation for use on educational and community regeneration programmes: for example, efforts to inculcate ties to the home region in early school years so that attendance at university or college is an occasion for young persons to acquire the skills to prosper locally, not, as is now the case, a "first stage" in the exploration of the outside world that ends in emigration.

Two rural partnerships known to have reacted thoughtfully and effectively to local change are described below.

Ballyhoura Development Partnership

The Ballyhoura area straddles the Ballyhoura Mountains in the southeast of County Limerick and the northeast of County Cork. It is an agricultural area mainly dependent on small-scale livestock farming. In recent years it has experienced severe economic and employment problems. As a result, there has been an increase in the traditionally high rate of out-migration. Between 1981 and 1986, 1 100 people out of a total population of only 37 400 migrated from the area. The rate of unemployment is also high for a rural area, reaching 15 per cent in 1994. An increasing number of villages are derelict or at risk of becoming so.

The Ballyhoura Development Company grew out of the Ballyhoura Failte Soci- ety Ltd., which was created in 1986 as a co-operative venture with the objective of developing tourism as a source of rural employment. The initiative developed from a plan to regenerate the town of Kilfinane. In 1988, the initiative was extended into a broader rural development programme with the establishment of the Ballyhoura Development Board. It qualified for funding under the LEADER programme in 1992.

The development strategy of Ballyhoura Development has two main elements: enterprise promotion and community regeneration.

Community regeneration

According to local people, despite the remarkable range of local community groups, the spirit of community had begun to weaken. This was partly a result of new agricultural practices (notably measures introduced under the Common Agri- cultural Policy) that seemed to reduce the need for strong local co-operation and partly because of the apparently arbitrary and short-term support for community activities from the central government.

In the early 1970s there was a period of prosperity linked to the arrival of EU agricultural support mechanisms, but this has been followed by a more gradual decline in income levels as subsidies have been systematically reduced. During the 1970s and 1980s, community groups went into a period of relative inactivity. Two specific features of the CAP were noted by rural communities as contributing to this decline.

- First, the CAP helped the individual farmer, and more specifically larger farmers. It was not a programme of wider development of the rural area. Fundamentally, income in the area was channelled to individuals rather than to organisations that could plan strategically.

- Second, the CAP's quotas and intervention prices meant that farmers' incentives and incomes were determined by an outside agency on an individual basis. The sense of co-operation among farmers thus diminished as yields became conditional not on support from other farmers repaid in kind, but on directives outlining set-aside levels and so on.

The surge in out-migration, underemployment, and poverty in rural areas that has resulted from continuing restructuring of the agricultural sector and the cutting of EU subsidies has reinvigorated the rural development debate. The Integrated Rural Development and LEADER Programmes (discussed in Chapter 3) were the first attempts to address the non-agricultural questions that had arisen through the decline of agriculture. The activities of these relatively small-scale programmes has illuminated the need for rejuvenation of the traditional voluntarism and community support that once underpinned daily life in these areas.

The approach taken by Ballyhoura and South Kerry, among others, has been described as an attempt to recreate the community movement of the 1940s inspired by Canon Hayes. Community Councils were established by Hayes to help bring services to communities (electricity, water, sewage, and social facilities). This is still seen as the heyday of rural voluntarism, and the model for today's initiatives.

The first practical step taken by Ballyhoura Development Ltd. in community regeneration was the establishment of a Community Consultative Committee (CCC) in 1990. By 1993, when the CCC had grown to encompass more than 30 voluntary groups, it took on its first major project. With technical expertise from University College Dublin, 500 volunteers carried out an audit that collected data on the skills of 21 777 adults and the resources of over one thousand settlements. The audit had two products: 1) information which was used by the community in integrated planning (1994-99); 2) and motivation for the communities that they could organise large and innovative projects within a partnership structure. The motivation outcome was particularly significant because of the feeling among many local people that their work was undervalued by government.

One small but illustrative initiative undertaken by Ballyhoura Development is its Community Housing Project, an intermediate step between council housing and home ownership in rural villages. Council housing for those on a low income usually involves a move to estates in the larger towns where the vast majority of public housing is concentrated. As was discussed above, these public housing estates concentrate acute poverty and deprivation. The future of the people in these areas is, at best, uncertain. The Community Housing project starts from the premise that low-cost housing should not require relocation out of the Ballyhoura area and that it would be positive for the society as a whole if people were given the option to remain in their home area rather adding to the urban problems described above.

The houses made available to local residents through this scheme are either new or renovated and located in small villages. Selection of tenants is made by the local authority and by the local community with the aim of creating a mix of people that will sustain the vibrancy of the community, with preference given to those on council housing waiting lists. Although this is a small programme, it suggests an innovative approach to stopping the cycle of out-migration that has affected areas like Ballyhoura for over a century. Such community regeneration programmes, of course, only make sense within a development strategy that creates economic activity to deter out-migration.

Enterprise development

As was discussed earlier, the development of non-traditional farming indus-tries or niche market products requires strong co-operation among a range of different actors. This is exemplified by the agricultural diversification and alternative enterprise creation activities of Ballyhoura Development.

The quota restrictions on traditional farming activities in the Ballyhoura area prompted Ballyhoura Development to look for new products that the company could market on behalf of local small farmers. The partnership structure of the board generated the initial idea: a representative of the large Dairygold Co-operative who sits on the Board of Ballyhoura Development suggested that seed potatoes, which the co-operative was importing at the time, could provide a steady source of income for local farmers.

Ballyhoura Development identified the logical partners for the operation and organised the division of labour according to competencies. For example, Dairygold Co-operative acts as the market partner, advising on demand level, quality stan-dards and so on. The Department of Agriculture provides quality control and dis-ease testing services, while the Department of Agriculture's research and training arm, Teagasc, provides training courses. Local community groups, including farmers groups, acted to build a consensus on cultivation and purchase procedures and to guarantee the use of certified seed, thereby reducing the risk of disease.

The farmers have now formed a small co-operative, which agrees on standards for growers and will invest in refrigerated storage facilities and quality management equipment to more fully commercialise the business.

One of the important lessons from this example is that a strategic approach to enterprise creation permits a system to be put in place in which all the logical steps are covered by one actor or another. The problems of targeting and quality are here resolved by the involvement of the large commercial enterprise. Technical issues are taken care of by the Department of Agriculture and the Teagasc. Co-ordination is a key requirement.

According to Ballyhoura Development, and other development actors, many current development projects are somewhat naive in the sense that they are undertaken without sufficient attention being paid to long-term demand, identification of relevant partners, or relative quality standards that will be in effect.

In addition to the development of new agricultural activities, Ballyhoura is also involved in promoting alternative farm enterprises. The attraction of the speciality food industry is easy to see. First, the products have a high value added and are usually processed from local raw food commodities. Second, the domestic market for such products, which was traditionally underdeveloped, has expanded enormously, in line with a general European pattern of increased consumer demand for high-quality foodstuffs. The lack of domestic demand that inhibited the growth of a speciality food stuffs industry has now increased greatly, with ease of transportation making the British and European markets more accessible.

At the same time, this increasing demand is also characterised by "fickleness", a constant demand for new products and different brands. The cost of product development therefore becomes a key issue. It is not enough to identify a market for ham with a particular cure or glaze, that market is dynamic and, for the small supplier, there is a need to constantly refine the product or be developing others. Therefore, although the speciality or processed food industry is attractive, it is also both competitive and demanding.

Ballyhoura Development are currently guiding the development of a number of alternative enterprises. Among the most successful is an enterprise specialising in cured meats. The would-be entrepreneur, who had been curing meats on a small scale for a long time, approached Ballyhoura with the idea of expanding production and selling commercially. Ballyhoura provided assistance with developing a business plan, researched the feasibility of curing on a large scale, and helped him find the best mix of cures for the national and international markets. With funding from the LEADER Programme, the entrepreneur was helped to define the level of expected income from the enterprise, the level of investment that could be supported and given some grant assistance to purchase buildings and cooking and smoking equipment. The enterprise has now identified a successful image and brand name for itself and has been successful in marketing its products to super-markets and other large distributors. However, as was mentioned before, the com-petitive nature of the market means that new products must be continuously developed and existing products refined.

It is in this area that the LEADER can play an important role. Providing investment capital to buy land or buildings may more properly be the role of the private financial sector, small business advising may be the role of Forbairt, but the provision of resources and guidance in such innovative areas as new product development, which is key to the successful adaptation and survival of small busi-nesses, is an area where a programme like LEADER comes into its own. The idea of a permanent research team to help local small enterprises respond to changes in demand was mentioned by one representative of Ballyhoura. Given the range of enterprises from cooked meats to goat's cheese that are faced with constant devel-opment and redevelopment of product lines, this would appear to be an idea that captures the spirit of the LEADER concept.

South Kerry Partnership

The South Kerry Partnership Limited is located in a remote rural area of southwest Ireland which has, for the past century and a half, suffered endemic out-migration. The root problem in the area, even today, is lack of a stable population base. The inhabitants of the region are spread over a wide area and there is not a sufficient critical mass to sustain traditional economic activities. The lack of job opportunities, however, both limits income possibilities for those who stay in the area and pushes others to emigrate. The official unemployment rate is therefore not particularly high. The partnership, whose mandate is to combat long-term unem-ployment, must address wider issues than those of retraining, insertion and so on. The primary objective of the partnership is population retention; the method identi-fied to achieve this is enterprise creation and regeneration of economic activity, allied with revival of community and cultural services.

The area poses the classic problems of finding non-agricultural rural activities that can generate reliable income in remote areas. The South Kerry Partnership, like other rural local development groups, is trying to exploit the potential of niche products, in particular speciality food products. As was mentioned earlier, the level of expertise in the development of value-added, processed and speciality foodstuffs has been lacking in Ireland for a variety of historical and socio-economic reasons. The traditional constraints on speciality food product development still exist – a small indigenous population, hence low domestic demand; an agricultural sector focused mainly on agricultural commodities for export; and a poorly developed culinary history leading to a dearth of genuine local specialities. But the partnership believes that this is changing, with more awareness of both tourist and export market demand.

Mariculture has particular potential for an area such as South Kerry because: 1) it has a high value-added component, 2) for environmental reasons, it needs to be located away from urban settlement and heavy industry, 3) it is relatively labour intensive, and 4) it has low import requirements and is sourced locally, producing spin-off employment.

The South Kerry Development Partnership, recognising the significance and potential of mariculture, initiated the Mariculture Programme which involves a Mariculture Training Programme and supports the work of a Mariculture Develop-ment Officer, financed by the partnership in conjunction with three local in-shore fishermen's co-operatives. The work of the partnership aims to complement the grant aid and technical assistance initiatives of the Irish Sea Fisheries Board which have increased in recent years.

The mariculture or aquaculture programme is mainly concentrated on scallop farming. The local scallop industry has been successfully established to the point that local actors are looking for ways to increase the value added retained in the local area through processing and direct marketing. The partnership is therefore putting resources into market research and the development of local brand names and images.

At the same time, new shellfish stocks are being developed, in particular lobsters, oysters, and clams, and the partnership will be committing resources to further stock enhancement programmes. Financial aid is also being given to develop "demonstration" products whose feasibility on a large scale will then be assessed. Once it becomes clear that, for example, the purity of the waters around South Kerry is a suitable image around which to build a lobster or oyster farming industry, then the partnership, working through the contacts of the Mariculture Development Officer with the Fisheries Board, will look for additional governmental funding sources.[63]

In the development of the local mariculture industry, the South Kerry Partner-ship sees its role as supporting innovative activities which fall between the normal government funding channels. The partnership format provides a link with govern-ment that is essential in the elaboration of projects under the Mariculture Develop-ment Initiative – for example, the partnership's Mariculture Officer benefits from access to expertise and resources provided through the Fisheries Board even though the projects undertaken may be too small to qualify for direct grant support. Links with established professional business service providers such as Forbairt are particularly important in terms of advice and technical support.

The partnership is unusual because it combines both an Area-Based Partnership and a LEADER company. The combination of the two allows a broader and more flexible approach to promotion of economic projects than would be possible through a partnership alone even where social service provision has an equally high priority.

In terms of financing, the partnership programme has limited funds and a wide range of responsibilities. Even with an emphasis on promoting the economy of the region, the social needs of residents must also be catered to. In particular, essential services that have been slowly withdrawn from public provision on the grounds of insufficient population are often offered through the partnership. Despite the increasing emphasis of the programme on the merits of brokerage rather than direct service delivery, the reality of many rural areas is that there is no clear partner with whom to act as a broker in the absence of state agencies. The partnership has a certain obligation, therefore, to step in to provide some of the services that local people need on a day-to-day basis. It was mentioned to the OECD team that the high profile of the partnership in the local community depends on them taking clear action in favour of the local population over what are clearly stated needs. The provision of such services, which directly promote population retention but only indirectly impact upon the economy, demands the resources and time of the partnership. Given the limited financial resources of the partnerships, promotion of the economic life of the area through direct enterprise creation would be difficult without input from the LEADER programme.

The LEADER I Programme was particularly strong as a support for enterprise creation strategies in rural areas, particularly in terms of providing flexible grant aid. As such, it is a solid complement to the partnership in this South Kerry context. The partnership addresses the social agenda, while the LEADER company involves itself with the economic agenda. Moreover, the LEADER Programme is often a more flexible funding source in working with the partnership than state agencies have tended to be. For example, it was noted by many people living in the more remote communities that the OECD group visited that the centralised nature of the public administration (and the economy) led to national regulations having perverse effects in areas distant from Dublin. The partnership decided to establish a printing enterprise in the area, where it was thought tourist hotels and restaurants would provide steady business. Their application for support from the IDA was refused on the grounds that, as a sector, the printing industry was already saturated. Although as a national strategy sectoral targeting is a necessary element of industrial policy and offers safeguards against displacement effects, in this local situation it takes little account of the territorial dimension. Oversupply of a product in Dublin does not indicate oversupply in South Kerry. Regardless of whether the decision of the IDA was correct in economic terms, the LEADER Programme offers the partnership some ability to support small enterprise projects without the obligation to justify actions in terms of national policy strategies.

There is a strong sense in areas such as South Kerry that the government's policy overemphasizes urban industrialisation and that other policies are introduced at the margins without the same conviction and energy as goes into higher policy priorities. Perhaps, at heart, the issue centres around the lack of a regional policy, or the suspicion that regional policy consists of promoting the Dublin region and assuming that nothing can be done for areas like Kerry.

FROM THE PARTICULAR TOWARDS THE GENERAL

Incomplete as they are, the preceding reports suggest broad conclusions regarding both the partnerships' identification of new possibilities in the Irish economy and the potential for disadvantaged persons to participate in them. They also draw attention to the strengths and weaknesses of the partnerships as organisational instruments for making such discoveries, and making the most of them. Here, we draw out those generalisations, beginning with a review of the substantive findings. These will not surprise the participants in the partnerships, who seem to take them largely for granted; but they may together astonish outside observers, for whom the surprise may be that the partnerships assume the things they assume. Then we turn to certain aspects of the inner life of the partnerships, and in particular the sources and threats to the solidarity that has been a precondition of their effectiveness. To the surprise, perhaps, of no one who has tried to make important, small changes in a large and powerful world, we will conclude that as vigorous and successful as they have been, the partnerships are unlikely to survive their discoveries unless their relation with their broader environment is stabilised. Discussion of that task is reserved for the final chapter.

A new and accessible economy?

Reduced to a phrase, the finding contained in the experience of the Irish partnerships is that the new, decentralised economy is more pervasive and more accessible than normally supposed. It was evident in the interest of the small Plato firms in Tallaght in ISO 9 000 and the other disciplines needed to participate in the new customer-supplier relations. Its influence was evident as well in the choice of niche, time-sensitive markets and, to varying degrees, in the internal organisation of Speedpak in Northside and Paksort and Eros in Dundalk; and evident, too, in the search for speciality agricultural and maricultural products in Ballyhoura and South Kerry. Its evidence is all the more surprising because Irish observers in a good position to know did not expect to find it, and had to convince themselves it could truly be there once the experience of the partnerships was reported to them. "More than previously thought", of course, is not the same as "a lot"; and by itself, the pervasive influence of the new economy on the projects we visited says little about the actual extension of the new economy in Ireland or elsewhere. It may even be the case that, following a suggestion in Chapter 2, the early and extensive Irish contact with multinationals changed at some point from a liability to an advantage as these firms began to experiment in earnest with the new methods, and that Ireland, far from being backward, or even just typical – whatever that means in this uncertain context – is in some ways ahead of the economic game. But taking all this into consideration, it seems nonetheless fair to conclude on the basis of the Irish experience that "Irish" surprises of improbable development may be lurking in many apparent backwaters, hidden by the mist of old expectations of stagnation.

On the Irish evidence, moreover, the new economy is not only more pervasive, but also more accessible to persons from low-wage communities than commonly thought. This is conspicuously so with respect to training programmes such as Paksort and Speedpak. They train persons from just those communities in work that demands the problem-solving skills and rigorous reliability that mark the "high performance" jobs said to be characteristic of the new, competitive economy. They do so – Speedpak more deliberately, Paksort less so – by mimicking the very conditions in the factory-classroom that the participants will find in the modern factory.

If the initial successes of projects like these can be sustained and generalised, they will compel reconsideration, in Ireland and elsewhere, of the nearly exclusive focus on questions of incentives and their effects on morals that have animated public and academic discussion of the connections among work, welfare, and training in recent years. The central and familiar argument in that discussion is that public support for the needy dulls the incentive to work and eventually creates a dependence on state aid that, in undermining the desire to be self-supporting, destroys first the intention and then the very capacity to acquire the skills needed for economic independence in modern life. Debate has accordingly focused on demonstrations that particular incentives or training schemes do or do not destroy the disposition to or the capacity for work. Once the key question became whether persons on welfare were in some large sense fit to work or not, there was no pressing reason to pay attention to changes in the organisation of work, and still less to look closely at the content and precise organisation of training programmes. If welfare recipients or members of their communities were losing the capacity to work, not much was added to the characterisation of the problem by saying just what sort of work they were decreasingly capable of doing. For good measure, however, the common assumption is that modern, high-performance jobs increasingly require just the autonomy and entrepreneurial self-determination that welfare saps. So the decreases in ability and motivation – disqualifying in themselves – are made more burdensome by an increase in the demands placed on "modern" workers.

But if high-performance work is becoming more prevalent, reaching areas of the economy previously regarded as frozen in a more rudimentary past, and if the long-term unemployed can meet the new demands placed on them, then questions of incentives aside, it is worth considering what training and other services ought to be provided to disadvantaged communities so that their members can make the most of the possibilities becoming available to them. Such consideration seems to be especially justified in the light of the recent findings in the US and elsewhere that the same group problem-solving techniques employed by firms are pedagogically effective in school settings because they establish a practical context – construction, say, of a scale model roof using a triangular frame which facilitates mastery of abstractions in trigonometry, for instance. The vocational schools that obtain the best results are, correspondingly, those that integrate the teaching of such subjects into projects that, as in Speedpak, in turn anticipate conditions in factories where disciplined problem solving has become the indispensable routine.[64]

The Irish evidence indicates that the new economy may be more accessible than previously thought in a second sense as well: the flurry of new ventures, in diverse sectors and with entrepreneurial protagonists from many walks of life, suggests the possibility that the image of the modern high-tech start-up launched by the highly educated and backed by the specialist venture capitalist may give an unduly narrow impression of the routes new firms take to the modern economy. At the very least, and less grandly, the evidence suggests that under certain circumstances economic development organisations can take on the functions of venture capitalists, providing expertise in business strategy and organisation along with access to capital and certification of a project's viability by their association with it.

The examples of the seed-potato project in Ballyhoura, mariculture in South Kerry, Speedpak in Northside, and Paksort and Eros in Dundalk all show that the partnerships are particularly good at providing this bundle of services. By mobilising and combining the expertise of the local managers and bankers, as well as the knowledge of the broader community of local needs and the abilities of the workhorse, the partnerships are well-placed to nurture and select promising ideas, finance ventures and help solve the problems they encounter early on. In any event, the partnerships are more accessible to and less daunting for would-be entrepreneurs with little managerial experience than institutions such as the County Enterprise Boards, Forbairt or Business Innovation Centres (BICs).

Whether these capacities can be formalised in enduring institutions is unknown. There is the possibility that the partnerships will inspire a kind of popular venture capitalism, opening entrepreneurship, to new circles in just the way the new kinds of training widen access to the new workplaces. But it is also possible that these activities will be brought low by the tension between the general mobilising required for the success of each entire project, and the assignments of the fruits of that broad effort to the few persons who own or come to be employed in the resulting firm. Why should all pool their knowledge, or, more pointedly, do with less support for their own projects so that others, selected behind closed doors, can be offered greater opportunities? The less favoured may forebear in their protest as their contribution to the extraordinary but exhausting – and therefore necessarily temporary – solidarity with which communities react to adversity. But if decisions regarding assistance to start-ups cannot become public enough to permit potential participants to convince themselves that the projects sponsored are the best ones and truly worthy of community support, not simply those favoured by particular sponsors or interests, forbearance will turn to rancour, and the solidarity needed for success will be disrupted by fights over the potential spoils.

The prospect of such fights presages broader and potentially paralysing conflicts between solidarity and self interest that could develop within the partnerships; and it is this tension, contained for now but menacing nonetheless, that we turn to next.

Commerce and community

The central political paradox of the partnerships is the dilemma of their incipient popular venture capitalism writ large. Resources, public and private, can be diverted from their current use to experiments with uncertain results only if there is a community consensus, founded on deep solidarity, to do so. But there is no assurance that the experiments will benefit the various groups in the community in proportion to either their contributions or their needs, especially since different groups will have differing estimations of what they have given and what they are getting in return. Different understanding of the purposes and potential benefits of local development are thus part cause and part effect of nascent disputes about the use to which experimental freedom should be put.

These differences are manifest first, and most generally, in the differing emphasis of partnerships of certain types of projects whithin a broadly integrated approach. PAUL, for instance, thinks of itself as more "socially oriented", and, as we saw, pursues activities aimed at improving the lot of those most dependent on various form of public assistance, particularly through legislative or administrative reform. Dundalk aims to help disadvantaged groups through a wide ranging programme of firm and employment creation. Given a choice, social welfare recipients in Dundalk might prefer PAUL's strategy, while potential entrepreneurs or unemployed persons seeking to develop their skills in Limerick might see more promise in the Dundalk approach. For now, of course, they do not have the choice, and the hope is that discoveries made pursuing the one strategy will complement the other, with the result that there will be no need to choose in the future.

A second manifestation of these differences is the division of labour within many partnerships between "business/economic" and "social/community" subcommittees of the board of directors, with perhaps a third subcommittee on training. As a rule, "economic" committees are charged with business development while the "social" committees are concerned with welfare policy, conditions in the housing estates, and the like. In theory, these activities are complementary as well; but the constituencies for each, and just as important, the orientations and, so to speak, the reflexive responses of the representatives on the respective committees are distinct, and often – quietly, for the moment – in tension.

Painted with a very broad brush, the members of the business committee are managers with a heart, but managers nonetheless: anxious to help the vulnerable help themselves (but impatient, perhaps, with those who start discussions by insisting on the right to help); used to results and conversations clearly focused on how to get them (and impatient, perhaps also, with people who lack their experience in managing many activities at once). They represent the sort of persons in the area who feel they have an obligation to give something back in return for all the things participation in the local community has given them – not least, of course, the recognition as a leader of the (business) community. Painted with the same broad brush, the persons on the social committee are community activists: of the community, thoughtfully and passionately aware of its problems, its hopes and its capacities – but political activists and consequently anxious to join a movement that creates hope of progress where there was little (but impatient with persons who seem to think, perhaps silently, that the community's problem is a lack of initiative and active optimism); ready to work for results (but willing to spend lots of time making sure they know what the goals are, and suspicious, perhaps, of those who always seem to have answers before questions are asked, and who seldom have the time for explanations when they are); ready to get down to brass tacks and say what are – for outsiders – brutally honest things about the debilitating effects of welfare dependence on the young (but very impatient with those who think the older, long-term unemployed could get jobs just by wanting them enough); anxious, above all, to participate, to take a step towards asserting joint control of a situation that seems beyond all deliberate influence (but short with those who hint that this participation is a favour granted in tough times, not a right of citizenship).

For the time being, the groups co-exist and co-operate with one another. For public purposes, in addressing the outside world of government agencies and politicians, they need each other. Together they do speak for the community, for they embody in miniature the social partnership recognised as legitimate in the nation as a whole. Separately, it is unclear that either, indeed any part of either, has anything like a formal mandate to speak for any broad interest, let alone the common one. Can the unions' nominee on the partnership board speak for the unemployed? for the unions? Those with whom we spoke did not claim to. Can the nominees of the Irish Business and Employers Confederation (IBEC) speak for "local business", for the IBEC? None pretended to. Can the community activists speak for the community as a whole, or just the group from which they come? Can they truly speak for that? None claimed legitimacy apart from a group; none asserted that group to be uniquely legitimate.

And they do work together. We were told again and again that the new training programmes and reforms in the welfare benefits rules, for example, would be unthinkable had the community groups not established open relations between the residents in the housing estates and the various administrative entities which, under normal circumstances, those residents would have avoided at any cost. But there is deeper collaboration too. By common consent, for instance, the managers of the new firms that hire the previously unemployed could not work with their employees as well as they do had they not first worked long and hard with their representatives.

But the co-operation achieves its balance through the momentum of success. If the partnerships lose their forward motion, and the promise of new and broader rewards that goes with it, the accounting will start, and before it is nearly done the co-operative balance will be disturbed. For, stopping now, it is easy to see how each group would calculate that it has contributed much and received rather little. The partnerships will avoid this reckoning only if their progress continues to make plausible the assumption that their joint efforts are indispensable to large and beneficial changes, not just locally, but in the organisation of national government as well. But the only way to establish the plausibility of that assumption is to establish a reliable, credible method for demonstrating to local constituencies and the national polity which projects are working, how to generalise them, and which should be stopped. Thus, paradoxically, the only way to avoid an abrupt reckoning that jeopardises all that has been done is to find a method to keep accurate track of what is working and what is not all the way along.

5

CONCLUSIONS

The partnerships that we have seen are extraordinarily innovative, but they have been better at creating new things than at building stable institutions that embody and extend their innovations. In part, this is because the Irish state has been better at allowing innovation than at learning from its protagonists about how to generalise local successes and incorporate changes they suggest into the organisation of the functional administration. Thus many experimental projects undertaken by the local development groups may succeed, but the experiment as a whole may fail. If we focus on the disparity between innovative promise and institutional reality, it is because the partnerships, like all efforts at concerted public action, will be judged less by the possibility of reform that they inspire than by the extent to which they enrich the routines of citizens and their representatives. Thus, although the reality may in fact be more benign, our conclusions deliberately assume a pessimistic view of the institutional climate in order to highlight ways to reinforce the structure as a whole.

Time for considered reform is short. So far the partnerships and their progeny have benefited from a limited and provisional dispensation from normal administrative and democratic controls because of the patronage of the Prime Minister's Office, the support of the social partners, and public recognition of the urgency of the problems they address. Shielded by this exemption, and adding to their national patronage the local political support that comes to the party "in motion", the partnerships have substantial informal power to direct funds from state agencies to the benefit of their own projects. In some areas, the regional directors of the state training and economic development authorities implicitly grant the partnerships authority to disburse funds allocated to their localities. Formal authority for the use of the funds continues, however, to rest with the functional agencies. It is hard to see how the agencies could make this temporary arrangement permanent without fundamentally redrawing their internal lines of authority.

Such instability is directly connected to questions regarding the partnerships' democratic legitimacy. Both as independent local entities and as the local mandatories of sub-national units of the central administration, they are, under felicitous circumstances, the complements and under normal conditions, the competitors of local government. But who are their constituents? How may citizens affected by their actions approve or reject what is done in their name? The partnerships were created in the image of national concertation among the social partners whose relation to the formal institutions of parliamentary democracy is no more clarified in Ireland than in the countries of Central and Northern Europe, where such concertation has been practised for decades. More troubling still, however consolidated and qualified they may be, the organisations participating in the partnerships' boards and projects can seldom claim to speak on behalf of all, or even the greater part, of the social groupings – tenants, women's groups, the unemployed – they represent. Thus they may lack at their own, local level the kind of self-evident legitimacy that would ease constitutional doubts about the place of the social partners in national policy making. In a democracy, practical success can never substitute for electoral review.

Finally, the general sense of the partnerships' precarity is heightened by the perceived ticking of the EU funding clock as it advances towards 1999. This ticking reminds the participants that the momentary stability they enjoy under the EU's Community Support Framework does not assure a stable future. The Government, which would be called on to accomodate budgetary shortfalls out of domestic tax receipts if EU funding were not extended, has expressed its support for the Area-Based Partnerships and local development in general. But how reliable would such support be if the claims of various local development efforts, many of uncertain administrative and political status, were weighed against each other and the general goal of fiscal restraint?

The partnerships are, in some areas, already engaged in justifying their authority and resources, particularly with regard to the local governments; in all the remaining areas, this is looming. The confusion of jurisdictions has also become an explicit concern to both parliament and the national administration. Within important functional agencies, there is concern about the extreme complexity of de facto administrative arrangements at the local level, and especially the profusion of new local entities with ill-defined and therefore possibly conflicting responsibilities. Various public agencies would be in a position to put forward a plan of consolidation and simplification should eventual conflicts demonstrate the need for such a plan. Presumably, state agencies with competing ambitions and anxieties have also prepared organigrams of their own, each of which is simplicity itself, viewed from the vantage point of the centre.

The government, for its part, convoked a Commission on Devolution in 1995 to consider rectification of the jumbled relations among various levels of government and local development groups. Although it is too early to judge the orientation of the Commission, it will, necessarily and rightly, mix the high politics of institutional reform with the everyday politics of position and place. To intentionally take the worst-case scenario, it, or an eventual successor, may simply declare the progammes over. Partnerships would then be placed under the purview of established authorities, and their freedom of action sharply reduced. The successful projects would then be amalgamated to various functional ministries or departments of local government, as the case may be, and subjected to the rules, however alien to their animating spirit, of their new supervisors. Whether they continued to exist formally or not, the partnerships would likely lose the charter to experiment through the creation of new projects which has been the well-spring of their inventiveness thus far.

But we do not think this is a necessary outcome. In the following section we discuss some of the elements that contribute to the institutional weakness of partnerships and look at ways to retain the vitality of the partnerships while clarifying and reinforcing their institutional place. We argue that the best way to do this is not to go from the outside in, by reordering their relation to other authorities, but rather from the inside out, with reform of the methods by which the project experiments themselves are monitored and evaluated. This alternative draws on firms' new techniques for linking the experimental exploration of possibilities to continuous revision of their original goals and the organisational means by which they are pursued. Turned to problems of collective, public action, we will call the ensemble of these innovations "democratic experimentalism"; and we will suggest how, applying their core method of self-evaluation through continuous and disciplined comparison, the projects and partnerships can learn from their successes and failures, render themselves accountable to their local constituents, offer credible guidance in the long-term reconstruction of national institutions, and thus invigorate the novel, socially inclusive concertation in which Ireland is now engaged.

To underscore the fragility of the current situation and the opportunity of a democratic experimentalist alternative, we begin by setting out shortcomings in the way the partnerships and projects exchange information horizontally, among themselves, and the related problems of vertical co-ordination between them and the central authorities and horizontal co-ordination with other local development groups.

THE CURRENT DIFFICULTIES OF HORIZONTAL AND VERTICAL CO-ORDINATION

Officially it is the responsibility of Area Development Management (ADM) Ltd., formerly the National Co-ordinating Team, to ensure the regular exchange of pertinent information among the partnerships and to act as an intermediary between the partnerships and the government. But the ADM is simply overtaxed. By all accounts, its capacities were stretched to the limit even when it was charged with supervision of the original twelve PESP partnerships. With the addition of 26 new ones, despite significant additional resources, the majority of ADM's efforts are currently devoted to the daily details of organising the new groups. ADM plans careful comparisons of the performance of partnerships with regard to particular areas of activity; but during this transitional phase, its ability to carry out these plans is limited.[65] However, despite these pressures, ADM is supporting the exchange of information through its liaison staff, who attend most of the partnership board meetings. ADM has also published a detailed handbook on local development and a series of resource materials on good practice. It has organised regional and national seminars for those participating in local development projects and has commissioned research on aspects of the work of partnerships, including support for community business. It is, however, the informal support through its liaison staff which provides the most valuable information exchange. ADM must ensure that the information gained informally is systematically applied.

Informal, episodic exchanges among the partnerships provide at best a partial and precarious substitute for formal co-ordination. Sometimes, of course, simple word of mouth does work. The diffusion of the Plato network from Tallaght to other partnerships is an example. But the disadvantages and limits of such informality are equally evident. The ideas in the wind may be those that are best marketed, not necessarily those with the greatest potential: recall that the Plato concept is actively promoted by a network of European affiliates. The Department of Enterprise and Employment's feasibility study on the expansion of Plato concluded that the process should be very gradual. However, the general clamour to be involved in such a high-profile project may quickly overtake more considered preferences for phased development. Good or bad, moreover, ideas transmitted informally or in marketing brochures are typically too sketchy to permit thorough discussion of how, if at all, they should be applied in the new setting. What is missing, crucially, is a rigorous assessment of what has been learned of their strengths and weaknesses in their original territory, and how these lessons might be made serviceable to others. For that reason, the establishment of an active network by the Partnerships themselves, and the creation of a Bureau to structure their interaction is timely.

The success of Plato in Tallaght apparently depends on the coexistence of large firms who have mastered the new industrial disciplines and many subcontractors interested in acquiring such expertise. The Plato method of networking may work well under other conditions as well; but it is fair to assume that the mentoring of small firms by large ones will not work everywhere – situations where large customers are shifting costs of adjustment to small suppliers come to mind – and the more thorough the discussion of the possibilities of emulation, the greater, plainly, the chances of success.

Above all, however, the limit of informal exchange is that it makes the diffusion of innovation hostage to chance. Many new ideas, regardless of whether they result from accidental variations of habit or a more deliberate search for new methods, are put to work solving practical problems long before their achievements are fully grasped by their promoters and can be explained to others. For example, Ballyhoura Development has an inchoate idea of a new kind of tourism, in which the tourists are invited to watch the rural economy at work, making, for instance, speciality foodstuffs or knitwear. The appeal of the concept is that it suggests a standard by which to balance the claims of development directed to tourism and development directed to furthering the rural economy. Forms of tourism that disrupt agriculture and by-employment (anything from sausage- and cheese-making to production of seed corn) are excluded, as are developments of agriculture or food processing that would destroy the rural harmony the tourists seek. Whether the idea is a useful guide to reflection and development in Ballyhoura, much less nearby South Kerry, remains to be seen. But no good is served, and some potential acceleration of the exploration of possibilities is surely lost, because South Kerry, reasonably enough, does not have any knowledge of an idea Ballyhoura is just beginning to formulate.

Similarly, the Northside Partnership had only sketchy knowledge of the Speed-pak project at Dundalk, and Dundalk had only sketchy knowledge of Paksort at Northside, even though the projects must count as the closest of cousins. Both projects are admittedly young, but in this case early, systematic exchange might have saved time and trouble for both, and set the stage for a continuing and mutually informative evaluation of results. No such exchange was contemplated.

The increasing heterogeneity of the partnerships and the growing complexity of their relations with other local entities, finally, will likely make the shortcomings of informality more and more burdensome. Already, our interlocutors said, the differences between the established partnerships and the newly created ones was sufficient to impede exchange between the two groups.

Related problems may limit the possibilities of exchanges between the partnerships and other entities. For example, the County Enterprise Boards – until now charged mainly with disbursing grants – are being asked to expand their scope and cooperate more closely with the partnerships within the context of the Operational Programme. In some cases, as noted above, this has resulted quickly in complementary relations. For example, the manager of the Northside Partnership is on the board of the Dublin City Enterprise Board and has obtained matching funding for Speedpak through the CEB. The role of the Limerick City Enterprise Board as the city-wide provider of grant aid and business advice allows the Partnership, whose mandate also covers the whole city, to focus on particularly deprived areas and the most marginalised groups. Often, however, the potential partners' respective ideas of what constitutes a "project" – a grant proposal for the County Enterprise Boards, a working group or subcommittee of the board devoted to a particular problem for the partnerships – means that collaboration between them is most difficult when it is most needed: early in the life of a new venture. Whether the Country Strategy Groups, established recently to co-ordinate economic and employment development activity at county level, will reduce such frictions or aggravate them by introducing another irregularly shaped body into the mechanisms of local government and politics is an open question.

Beyond these local confusions, vertical co-ordination between the partnerships and the central government is also faulty. As has been mentioned, ADM is still endeavouring to cope with the increase in the number of partnership groups. Nevertheless, ADM's insight is crucial, and through seconding staff to ADM, government agencies can have access to their overview. Separate administrative departments, such as FÁS or Forbairt, might remedy part of the defect, and indeed several government departments have established regular direct contacts with the partnerships. But to co-operate and learn from local activities the administrations would have to decentralise authority internally themselves, a slow and difficult process under any circumstances, and given the many imponderables of the situation – in particular, the uncertain future of the partnerships – it is not surprising that they have not been eager to pursue this course. For example, the same office that is charting the bewildering complexity of local administration and devising plans for its simplification also admitted that co-ordination among regional-level officials within its own organisation was weak.

Vertical communication between local development initiatives and central government is not, however, solely reliant on ADM. The Minister for Local Development meets regularly with representatives of the partnerships to discuss areas of common concern. The liaison team to support the County Strategy Groups is based in the Department of the Taoiseach. It provides a channel of communication for the local development organisations as they address their common concerns. The Departments of Enterprise and Employment and Agriculture, Food and Forestry also maintain close contact with CEBs and LEADER Groups, respectively. Other Government Departments and Agencies at national level have developed their own structured dialogue with local development actors. However, even if administrative departments, out of conviction or institutional self-interest, were to champion particular partnership programmes, the results could be limited. By including the programme in its catalogue of activities, the sponsor may detach it from complementary institutions or, more generally, isolate it from the local context of innovation on which its further development depends. The more the sponsor applies its standard criteria of effectiveness to the new programme, the less likely that distinctive features of that programme – those that suggest new possibilities and, as we will argue in a moment, new measures of performance – will survive review.

Under favourable circumstances, the social partners, particularly the unions, with their extensive contacts both within firms and among the unemployed, might have played the role of surveying and helping institutionalise promising local developments in areas such as training and job placement. However, the pressure of providing core services for members limits the capacity to support representatives on partnership boards. The lack of guidance, at least in the early period of their establishment, meant that social partner representatives were required to develop their own understanding of the role to be played. For the same reasons, social partners at national level face difficulty in identifying the implications of experience at local level.[66]

The effectiveness of both the statutory bodies and the social partners as conduits for ideas and innovations is also impaired by the profusion of local and regional committees with which they are associated. Representatives of the agencies and social partners typically serve on a number of different local development boards. Formal membership on one is no obstacle to membership on any number of others. But the more committees to which a single representative belongs, the less time can realistically be devoted to each, and to connecting any or all to the activities of the sponsoring organisation. While in theory, therefore, the board members' intimate knowledge of several groups should foster horizontal exchange, their knowledge is often acquired under conditions that reduce its utility.

The upshot is that the central government's mechanisms for systematically monitoring local developments with an eye to identifying projects worthy of general application (or, for that matter, plainly unworthy of continued support) appear, at least for the moment, inadequate. The social partners are ill-positioned to spring into the breach. And the partnerships, beset by their own problems of horizontal co-ordination, as well as day-to-day operations, cannot advance common and well-founded views on this question on their own. Whether particular local projects or programmes do come to be considered as exemplary in national debate depends, therefore, not so much on whether these projects and programmes have been validated by local experience as on the luck or skill of the local group in advocating its plans in national settings.

Advocacy more than accident accounts for the PAUL Partnership's success in introducing its proposals for reform, particularly in the area of rights for welfare recipients, into the national agenda. Indeed, such advocacy, we saw, has become one of the partnership's principal activities. PAUL's Money Advice Project had substantial influence on, for example, the Consumer Credit Bill and on a national financial advice scheme introduced by the Department of Social Welfare; various measures to enable the unemployed to retain benefit entitlements were based on recommendations made by the partnership; and the Social Employment Scheme's transformation into the Community Employment Scheme was influenced, among other inputs, by an evaluation of the SES carried out in Limerick by PAUL. The (potential) paradox, of course, is that to be an effective national advocate for its ideas, a local partnership must spend much of its time advocating those ideas nationally, not testing them locally.

'The results of a mixture of accident and advocacy would be small consolation for the opportunities missed for want of systematic discussion of the broad range of local innovations or of the starting points or the components of broader reforms.

There have, however, been examples of policy learning based on the monitoring of the experiences of partnerships. For example, the Community Employment Programme for the Long-Term Unemployed was based on the experience of a pilot programme (Community Employment Development Programme) operated in the pilot partnership areas. Similarly, their experience of a pilot Area Enterprise Allowance Scheme led to the introduction at national level of a Back to Work Allowance, which has proved highly successful. The Local Employment Service, being established to target the needs of long-term unemployment, draws heavily on the experience of the pilot partnerships, especially the Northside Partnership described earlier. However, programme monitoring is not sufficient.

Consider, as an illustration of what is currently missed, the situation of the Northside Partnership and Paksort. Whether Paksort is a model worth emulating; whether, rather, its distinctive features might usefully be incorporated into reform of the existing vocational training system, or yet again whether there is some fatal flaw in the method that has so far escaped attention, all this we cannot say. The results so far are encouragement enough to warrant serious investigation of these possibilities. But such is the haphazard nature of the discussion of innovations that a full airing of these matters appears inconceivable. Inconceivable is not hyperbolic here. Asked how they might extend their current project, our interlocutors took the question literally, and told us of plans to increase the floor space of the factory. Asked how the national authorities might help, they suggested by relaxing some of the welfare rules that make participation for some of their potential clients difficult. Asked more pointedly whether some part of the national training administration might take a helpful interest in their activities, they reported that none of the relevant officials had yet visited the facility.

There is, in line with the normal conditions governing Operational Programmes, provision in the Local Development Programme for independent evaluation of the performance and impact of the local development activity supported from European Structural Funds. Successful policy learning cannot be confined to formal evaluation. It is important, therefore, that evaluators engage on an ongoing basis with those implementing local development measures. The remainder of this chapter outlines a framework within which both evaluation and ongoing policy learning can maximise the benefit of the effort at local level.

THE PROJECT OF DEMOCRATIC EXPERIMENTALISM

A system of democratic experimentalism might correct these problems by applying to the partnerships, and public administration more generally, the methods of self-scrutiny validated in the new, decentralised firms. The core of these methods, we saw, is the continuous re-evaluation of means and ends in the light of comparisons of current designs and operations with potential alternatives, particularly through disciplines such as simultaneous engineering and benchmarking. The former focuses on relations within an organisation and the way innovations in one area of activity resonate with the understandings of others; the latter focuses on comparisons among institutions and their products either as wholes or parts. The joint effect of the application of these and related disciplines is to link detection of errors and insufficiencies to re-examination of assumptions of what is possible, and to do this in a way that renders each actor and institution accountable to its collaborators.

To envisage the application of these methods in the setting of the partnerships, think of each of them, together with the other institutions with which they collaborate, as producing for the local area a complex economic development and training service composed of discrete types of projects. Changes in a project such as, say, job training, suggest changes in the purpose and design of adjacent ones, such as job-placement or grant programmes that encourage welfare recipients to seek employment. Cumulatively, these revisions can lead to a redefinition of the purposes of the partnership company as a whole. Systematic discussion in public administration of the advantages and disadvantages of various combinations of the possible adjustments would be the equivalent to the analysis by simultaneous engineering of the relation of changes proposed in some of the modules of a car design to eventual modifications in the others.

Similarly, projects undertaken in one partnership in an area such as employment training can be compared to like projects undertaken by other partnerships, and the general designs of similar partnerships – for example, how each organises the internal discussion of project modifications – can be compared as well. Systematic evaluation of the strengths and weaknesses of projects and partnerships in relation to others of the same kind is the equivalent in public administration of benchmarking the performance of one module or make of car by comparison to the competition. Thus, in public institutions, as in private firms, changes in the parts of the product and organisation that outperform the best current alternative, internal or external, would gradually lead to changes in the corresponding wholes; and these encompassing changes, again tested against the most attractive alternatives, would prompt the next round of partial reform.

Applied in this way, the new disciplines confound the distinction between co-ordination by market and co-ordination by bureaucratic means. In firms, they permit a finer-grained exploration of possibilities than is available using the price mechanism alone. Indeed, far from determining choices, the discussion of new customer-supplier relations showed that prices in the new decentralised firms set boundary conditions on discussions of alternatives organised by the immediate collaborators themselves. In this sense the new disciplines advance "market" ends by "administrative" means. In public administration, conversely, they introduce the compelling comparisons of performance normally associated with competition to extend the scope and heighten the urgency of public agencies' self-reflection. In this setting, therefore, they advance "bureaucratic" purposes by "market" means. Institutions that make "markets" more like "administrations", and vice versa can plainly not be reduced in their field of action to either; indeed we can raise – but not explore – the possibility here that, applied to both markets and administrations, these disciplines may eventually lead to a convergence in the steering mechanisms of realms long operated according to distinct principles.

How, if at all, the partnerships might make use of these disciplines to learn from what they do, is, for reasons inherent in the advantages of decentralisation itself, best left to them and the institutions associated with them. But by way of illustration of the general principles of a democratic experimentalism solution to their current difficulties, we suggest two types of organised comparisons: the first directed at benchmakring individual projects; the second at benchmarking the designs of partnerships as wholes, and especially their methods of assessing and adjusting the fit of their various activities.

Thus the first comparisons would be concerned with projects of similar kinds – those aimed at, for example, teaching problem-solving in teams, matching potential employees to jobs, encouraging, evaluating, and financing proposals for new ventures, or supporting those financed. As a preliminary step, the partnerships, acting under the aegis of the central authority, and with the participation of the relevant board members, managers, and constituent groups, would decide which projects are to be treated as comparable. On reflection, job placement or creation in rural settings might be so different from analogous activities in urban ones that rural-urban comparisons are misleading, while the experience of urban and rural projects grouped separately is informative. Or it might be that urban projects of a certain type are themselves best divided into subgroups. In no case would a part-nership be required to assign all its projects to some comparison group from the start. This leaves room for experimentation outside familiar categories. But in no case, either, would a partnership be able escape scrutiny by declaring its core activities to be incomparably particular to its local setting.

The next steps, following directly from this categorisation, would be to characterise various ways of providing a particular service and the amounts pro-vided and to establish measures of successful performance. With both in hand, it would be possible to detect which variants of the general type of project perform best, and adjust accordingly. Thus in the case of programs aimed, for example, at teaching problem-solving in groups, projects might be distinguished by the compo-sition of the class. More older than younger students, or an even balance? Many participants with substantial work experience or few? Additionally, or alternatively, the projects might be grouped according to the relation each establishes between learning directed toward work-related problems and learning concerned with basic disciplines such as reading or mathematics. Are lessons in both presented within the same day or week, or is one regarded as a precondition for the other? Either way, how is work-based instruction co-ordinated with disciplinary or basic skills learning? Beyond such baseline statistics as placement rates, the outcome measures would be derived from careful analysis of the reactions of employers and managers who hire and supervise the project graduates, and teachers who encounter them later. Their judgements, connected to the original characterisation of the way the project provides its service, show which ways of organising learning in teams are most conducive to working in teams in various settings.

The second kind of comparison concerns the architecture of the partnerships as wholes or substantial parts. At the most general level, is each addressing the problems and actors appropriate to its particular setting? Or, more narrowly, are the organisations it deploys in some encompassing area such as training and job placement co-operating effectively amongst themselves and with other organisations, local and national, pursuing complementary ends? Again the first step would be exploratory self-categorisation. Partnerships would be classed in groups whose members regard themselves as co-operating in comparable activities. It might be held, for example, that training and economic development is a core complex of many, if not all partnerships. In urban settings these might embrace the efforts of institutions such as technical and vocational schools, welfare services, FÁS and Forbairt, unions and trade associations, and banks; in rural settings, producer co-operatives might play a larger role and unions a smaller one.

And, as before, the next steps would be to characterise activities and outcomes so as to allow an evaluation of performance. Here, however, the focus would not be on the features and contributions of individual projects, but rather on the patterns of co-operation among them and other institutions providing related services, and on indicators of the effectiveness of various patterns. In some cases, for example, co-operation among institutions might be wholly informal; in others, the institutional partners might have seats on one another's governing boards, establish distinct budgets for joint working groups, second the employees of one to the other, exchange information on a regular basis, or even co-ordinate long-range planning, and so on. The effective patterns will be those providing a flow of information and resources that increase the chances for success of established projects and create possibilities for new ones that could not otherwise be undertaken; ineffective relations among the project institutions will produce disorientation and conflict that hamstring operations at every turn. Thus if the training institutions have good knowledge of which local firms are themselves introducing team production or about to, they are more likely to place graduates of projects teaching problem-solving skills; and those graduates, once employed, can pass on information regarding the most suitable preparation for employment by participating in advisory groups convoked by their schools. Banks with current knowledge of which groups of firms, training institutions, and government agencies are adopting the new disciplines, and how effective these disciplines can be, presumably learn to value projects that cannot be collateralized by traditional means; and by extending credit to such firms they encourage the expansion of the innovative ensemble as a whole. Self-reinforcing relations of this kind might register, for example, the flow of persons from training institutions to jobs of a particular kind, or, in the reverse, flow of equipment or advisory personnel from firms to training programmes they seek to support; or, again, in the diffusion of equipment or techniques from demonstration projects in public technology consultancies and from schools to firms with whom they are working. Taken together, such assessments would indicate how well partners who need to co-operate in fact do co-operate, and by which institutional arrangements co-operation is achieved .

By proceeding in this way, monitoring and evaluation shifts from a review of local or regional subordinates' performance by national or supra-national superiors to a (disciplined) discussion of whether each part of the organisation is playing its role in advancing the purposes of the whole. In effect, each level and component of the complex of local service-providing institutions becomes accountable to the others and to its own immediate public. Projects that show badly in comparisons can be bluntly criticised by the partnerships and local and national governments that support them. But partnerships and communities that do badly in comparisons can be criticised just as bluntly by project managers, *their* constituents, and, of course, the citizens of the area. Both kinds of comparison will allow excluded groups to question the self-serving of entrenched interests if their arrangements are in fact obstructive. Finally, if the partnerships fail to agree on groups and methods of comparison, or fail to make a compelling demonstration of progress as measured by the methods they agreed upon, then the central government and *its* constituency will be in a position to judge their relative effectiveness. Just this kind of institutional discussion, we argue in conclusion, can provide an interim solution to the partnerships' immediate problems, while in the long run extending and reinforcing the novel form of socially inclusive concertation to which Ireland is committed.

TOWARDS A NEW FORM OF SOCIAL INCLUSION?

The partnerships' immediate problems, as we saw at the outset of this chapter, derive from their fragile democratic legitimacy and anomalous administrative status. Here we make explicit what was implicit there. Efforts to normalise the partnerships by subordinating them to the national agencies or incorporating them in local or county governments risk debilitating the former without strengthening the latter. The agencies of the national government are too fragmented and centralised to provide effective local co-ordination of current programmes, let alone to devise new ones. Local government is too limited in its scope, constrained in its capacities, and characterised by traditional approaches to oversee within its jurisdiction the effective redeployment of resources provided by the centre. If the only possibilities were to let the partnerships proceed by their own lights or place them under the tutelage of established institutions, Ireland would face a Hobson's choice.

The alternative is to increase substantially the public accountability of the partnerships without restricting their freedom of manœuvre; and this is just the combination of features that democratic experimentalism creates. Instead of forcing a vote, up or down, on the advisability of continuing on the current path of reform, democratic experimentalism shifts discussion to evaluation of the advantages or disadvantages of all the variants of co-ordinating local development in relation to national administration that have emerged in the profusion of the partnerships' activities. How, precisely, are County Enterprise Boards and partnerships configured when they work well together in various environments? Which connections between partnerships, local government, and national agencies work best under what conditions? In this discussion, the experience of the partnerships becomes a mirror in which to view the capacities of the variants of local administration, and vice versa. The more attentive that discussion is to variations in practice, furthermore, the more accountable all the actors become to their constituents. The more citizens know of developments beyond their home areas, the less likely they are to accept on faith the argument that local arrangements are uniquely suited to local particularities. "Simplifying" government in the light of such informed discussion would mean reforming it incrementally as a whole, not deciding which of the current pieces ought to be favoured over the others. Through democratic experimentalism, heightened accountability would lead to democratically legitimate and orderly institutions while protecting the polity against the risks of ill-defined authority.

For similar reasons, democratic experimentalism seems an indispensable complement to concertation of the new Irish type. The advantage of that concertation, we saw, is to provide a defensible guarantee of the living conditions of the most vulnerable while creating a stable environment for participation in an open economy and encouraging local innovation in the use of public resources. The obvious disadvantage is that certain localities, because of some combination of more favourable initial conditions and a surer hand at innovation, may consistently outperform others. In time, the guarantee of social inclusion could come to seem a pretext for toleration of ever greater regional disparities, and disregard for the fate of fellow citizens could be reconciled with the new definition of national solidarity.

But surely, within the context of concertation, the most direct way to reduce such disparities from the beginning or to decide what to do should they eventually emerge is to exchange detailed information regarding the successes and failures of local initiatives. The sooner dead-ends are discovered and thoroughfares extended, the less likely that any area will suffer a setback. Progress in one region would spur on the others, and reduce the chances that citizens anywhere would be victimised by the economic ignorance or self interest of local elites. The richer and more disciplined the exchanges, moreover, the easier it would be to identify the national rules and institutions that obstruct progress, and begin to elaborate ones that will foster it. The same goes for the organisation of the social partners themselves. The more, for example, that trade unions learn about the effective patterns of co-operation between their representatives on partnership boards, their representatives in local firms and their national headquarters, the better able they will be to determine whether the current distribution of authority between headquarters and the local branches of their own organisations is well suited to current conditions or not. Thus, in the long run, democratic experimentalism can contribute to the redefinition of the core institutions of concertation and to a new understanding of its purposes and possibilities.

Finally, with a glance towards a more distant future, we aver that the institutions and arguments presented here may have a place beyond Ireland's borders. Ireland is to the EU Structural Funds as any partnership is to the Irish government and the EU: one beneficiary among many of a programme designed to foster decentralised innovation. Presumably, Ireland's use of the EU funds could be compared to the use of such funds by other country recipients in just the way that partnerships can be compared – project by project or as architectural wholes – with each other. Indeed, the more the EU unifies its member economies and opens them to the world, the more social equity may well be seen, as it is implicitly in Ireland today, as the equitable development of areas and regions; hence, the more urgent such comparisons could become.

But such perspectives aside, the lessons of Irish experimentalism stand alone. A small country, in extremis, determines to find a way to reconcile economic growth with social equity when a long history of cautious pessimism and a recent past of discord might have counselled a more timorous strategy. The delegation of authority to local partnerships charged with connecting economic development with assistance to vulnerable groups reveals that the new, decentralised economy is more pervasive and more accessible to the vulnerable than had been assumed. But having overturned expectations and institutional routines, the partnerships have yet to fix their innovative activity in a form that both allows them to learn from what they do and renders them accountable to those they serve. To accomplish that, they and allied institutions would have to apply to relations among themselves, and to their projects, the same disciplines that they have learned through association with the local economy, and in which they are currently instructing firms and trainees. Whether and by what means this can be done is uncertain. But whatever its ultimate outcome, the Irish experiment in socially inclusive localism has, like all truly successful experiments, reassured its originators by demonstrating that there was something to find where they were looking, and bewildered them – and onlookers, too – by the promising complexity of the findings.

NOTES

1. Local authorities lost the power to levy local domestic rates in 1977.

2. This discussion centred largely around the work of the National Economic and Social Council, in particular the report *A Strategy for the Nineties,* to which both representatives of government and the social partners contributed.

3. This account follows closely the discussion by O'MALLEY, E. (1992), "Problems of Industrialisation in Ireland", in *The Development of Industrial Society in Ireland,* J.H. GOLDTHORPE and C.T. WHELAN, eds., Oxford University Press for the British Academy, Oxford, pp 31-52. See also, KENNEDY, Kieran A., "The Context for Economic Development", pp 5-30 (same volume).

4. O'MALLEY, E. (1989), *Industry and Economic Development: The Challenge of the Latecomer,* Gill and Macmillan, Dublin, p. 31.

5. See especially, CROTTY, R. (1986), *Ireland in Crisis: A Study in Capitalist Colonial Underdevelopment,* Brandon Book Publishers, Dingle.

6. For an account of the development and implications of this "possession mentality", see LEE, J.J. (1989), *Ireland 1912-1985: Politics and Society,* Cambridge University Press, Cambridge.

7. See MEENAN, J.F. (1970), *The Irish Economy Since 1922,* Liverpool University Press, Liverpool.

8. OECD (1992), *Industrial Policy in OECD Countries, Annual Review,* Paris.

9. OECD (1992).

10. See SHIRLOW, P., "Transnational Corporations in the Republic of Ireland and the Illusion of Economic Well-Being", in *Regional Studies,* Vol. 29:7, p. 687.

11. SHIRLOW, p. 689, Capital transfer pricing cannot, of course, account for differences in employment creation in which foreign multinationals have consistently out-performed indigenous industries.

12. See Industrial Policy Review Group (1992), *A Time for Change: Industrial Policy for the 1990s,* Government Publications, Dublin.

13. OECD (1993), *Economic Survey: Ireland,* Paris.

14. OECD (1995), *Labour Force Statistics, 1973-1993,* Paris, pp 268-269.

15. SABEL, C.F. (1994), "Learning by Monitoring: The Institutions of Economic Monitoring", in *Handbook of Economic Sociology*, Neil SMELSER and Richard SWEDBERG, eds., Princeton University Press-Sage, Princeton, pp 137-165.

16. See K. CLARK, T. FUJIMOTO, and W. B. CHEW (1987). *Product Development in the World Auto Industry*. Brookings Papers on Economic Activity 3, Washington DC, pp. 729-776.

17. See SMITKA, M.J. (1991), *Competitive Ties: Subcontracting in the Japanese Automobile Industry*, Columbia University Press, New York.

18. This section is drawn from a report written by David Jacobson for the OECD, in the context of the deliberations of a Working Group brought together by the NESC in autumn 1995. JACOBSON, D., "New Production, Organisation and Industrial Relations: An Annotated Bibliography," unpublished report for the OECD/NESC.

19. MURPHY, D. and B. LEAVY (1994), "Strategic Partnerships," paper presented at the 1994 Irish Production and Inventory Control Society Conference. (David Murphy is a manager at Amdahl.)

20. FYNES, B. and S. ENNIS (1994), "From Lean Production to Lean Logistics: Providing Manufacturing and Service Quality from a Peripheral Location", University College Dublin, Centre for Quality and Service Management, Working Paper No. 94:3. For Intel, see, CASEY, T. (1994), "Skill Transfer Mechanisms to and in a Less Favoured Region", in *Competitiveness, Growth and Job Creation – What Contribution Can Education and Training Make? Reports from the 1994 Cumberland Lodge Conference, Target*, R.D. PETTS and H.J. SCHMEHR, eds.

21. MOYNIHAN, M. (1994), "Strategic Alliances and Sub-contracting", paper presented at the 1994 annual conference of IPICS. (Moynihan is responsible for sub-contract procurement at Apple in Cork.)

22. See JACOBSON, D. and D. O'SULLIVAN (1994), "Analyzing an Industry in Change: The Irish Software Manual Printing Industry", *New Technology, Work and Employment*, Vol. 9, No. 2., and continuing research reported by Jacobson.

23. CASEY, T. (1994), "Skill Transfer Mechanisms to and in a Less Favoured Region", in *Competitiveness, Growth and Job Creation*, R.D. PETTS and H.J. SCHMEHR, eds.

24. For a discussion of the small firm sector, see KILLIAN, D. (1994), *Modern Production Management Systems in Small and Medium Enterprises: Barriers to Their Adoption and Implementation*, unpublished MBS dissertation, Dublin City University.

25. See, for example, Lucas Engineering & Systems (n.d.), "A Business Fit to Grow: Dublin Fine Meats", a brochure providing a case study of Lucas's work with Dublin Fine Meats over a ten-month period.

26. National Economic and Social Council (NESC) (1993), *A Strategy for Competitiveness, Growth and Employment*, Dublin, p. 252.

27. McCALL, B. (1995), "The Winning Side", *Enterprise and Innovation*, Vol. 1, No. 4.

28. MURPHY, M. (1995), *Strategies for Success: Servicing the Needs of Small to Medium Sized Enterprises*, FÁS Planning and Research Division.

29. SINNOTT, E.A. (1994), *Customer Service in Selected Irish Organisations: Theory and Practice*, unpublished Ph.D. dissertation, University College Galway.

30. This is particularly surprising because at the national level this issue has been the subject of a number of policy papers by the Irish Congress of Trade Unions and ICTU and the employers' association IBEC made a joint declaration on the need for greater employee involvement.

31. BUCKLEY, F., E.A. SINNOTT and K. MONKS (1995), "Implementing Quality Initiatives in Irish Organisations: Some Hidden Outcomes", unpublished typescript, Dublin City University Business School.

32. JACOBSON, D., "New Production, Organisation and Industrial Relations: An Annotated Bibliography", unpublished report for the OECD/NESC. For the European Foundation view, see FRÖHLICH, D., C. GILL and H. KRIEGER (1993), "Roads to Participation", *Workplace Involvement in Technological Innovation in the European Community*, Vol. I, European Foundation; and GILL, C., T. BEAUPAIN, D. FRÖHLICH and H. KRIEGER (1993), "Issues of Participation", *Workplace Involvement in Technological Innovation in the European Community,* Vol. II, European Foundation.

33. The operating guidelines transmitted to the partnerships by the Department of the Taoiseach were:

   • to work with people who are long-term unemployed and those in danger of becoming long-term unemployed in order to improve their skills and self-confidence, their involvement in the community, and their opportunities of getting a job or starting their own business;

   • to promote the type of fundamental attitudinal change needed to enable individuals to generate enterprise thereby creating additional employment and to encourage a more positive attitude towards the recruitment of people who are long-term unemployed;

   • to work at the local level to generate more jobs through sustainable enterprises and through the promotion of local economic projects and initiatives which will stimulate confidence and investment. Source: Area Development Management Ltd.

34. BLACKWELL, John (1988), *A Review of Housing Policy*, NESC Report, NESC, Dublin.

35. BLACKWELL, p. 156-57.

36. An evaluation of the People Against Unemployment in Limerick (PAUL) partnership, whose activity we will examine in the next chapter, put the widespread dissatisfaction with the coordination of national policies as follows:

   [The work of the partnership has shown how a] combination of poor planning practices, ill-considered housing policies and unequal educational opportunities are exacerbated by rapid and negative changes in the labour market. Meanwhile, the response of the State authorities has been neither fast nor imaginative enough. PAUL's experience challenges Ireland to view itself as an urbanised society, as well as a rural and provincial one, and to adopt an integrated range of urban development policies. In doing so, PAUL isolates the elements for such an urban policy: local estate management, adult education, legitimisation of the shadow economy, self-employment, small and medium-sized enterprise creation, investment in the physical infrastructure and consumer sensitivity in welfare services.

Combat Poverty Agency (1994), *Combating Exclusion*, p. 120.

37. The following draws extensively on Rory O'DONNELL and Colm O'REARDON (1996), "Irish Experiment: Social Partnership Has Yielded Economic Growth and Social Progress," *New Economy*, Vol. 4, No. 1.

38. See NESC (1986), *Strategy for Development*, Dublin.

39. By any measure, social partnership helped produced a remarkable improvement in Ireland's public finances. The general government deficit fell from 8.5 per cent of GDP in 1987 to 2.3 per cent in 1994. The ratio of gross debt to GDP declined to 91 per cent in 1994. Inflation fell, and remained well below the EU average. Under the PNR and its successors, moreover, collective bargaining agreements have been reached largely without conflict, and the number of strike days has fallen considerably. See Rory O'DONNELL and Colm O'REARDON, "Irish Experiment," *New Economy*. Since the PNR was signed, the Irish economy as a whole has performed extraordinary well. Even given the downturn in world markets in the early 1990s, GNP grew at an annual rate of 4.1 per cent between1988 and1994. Whereas total employment fell 0.82 per cent annually between 1980 and 1987, it increased by over 1.35 per cent annually between 1987 and 1990 and by 1.2 per cent per annum between 1991 and 1994. Manufacturing output in Ireland is growing at a rate of 7.5 per cent annually, which is the highest in the OECD and several times higher than the OECD average. Between 1986 and 1994, the annual growth rate of Ireland's manufactured exports was 9.9 per cent, putting Ireland in this regard among the best performers in the OECD, and just marginally behind the four major Asian Newly Industrialising Economies. How much of this success can be attributed to stabilization and how much to the structural changes discussed in Chapter 2 is, of course, hard to say.

40. See NESC (1991), *A Strategy for the Nineties*. Dublin.

41. See HARDIMAN, N. (1988), *Pay, Politics and Economic Performance in Ireland 1970-87*, Clarendon Press, Oxford.

42. TEAGUE, P. (1995), "Pay Determination in the Republic of Ireland. Towards Social Corporatism?", *British Journal of Industrial Relations*, 33:2, June.

43. See OECD (1990), *Partnerships for Rural Development*, Paris; O'MALLEY, E. (1992), "The Pilot Programme for Integrated Rural Development, 1988-90", Paper No. 27, *ESRI Broadsheet Series*, ESRI, Dublin.

44. See KEARNEY, B., G.E. BOYLE and J.A. WALSH (1994), *EU Leader I Initiative in Ireland. Evaluation and Recommendations*, Department of Agriculture, Food and Forestry/ Commission of the European Communities, Dublin.

45. Although the programme was expanded nationwide in 1993, its funding base remained limited pending the outcome of negotiations for the Community Support Framework. These were concluded in 1994 and provide support for the new entities until 1999.

46. Government of Ireland/European Commission (1995), *EU Operational Programme for Local, Urban and Rural Development 1994-1999*, Government Publications, Dublin, p. 47.

47. The newer CEBs (for example, those in Dublin) are currently taking on managers not directly connected to local government, with the aim of developing their range of services beyond that of administering grant support programmes. This evolution in the choice of personnel and the expansion in the scope of activities parallels developments in the British Training and Enterprise Councils.

48. See NESF *Report No. 2* which deals specifically with local development and the *NESC's New Approaches to Rural Development*.

49. Government of Ireland/European Commission (1995), *Operational Programme for Local Urban and Rural Development*, Government Publications, Dublin, pp 108-109.

50. Note the consideration given to strategies of "social learning" and "social reform" and a trend toward social mobilisation and negotiational local planning that has been identified in many OECD countries at the moment.

51. KELLY, Sarah (1994), *Progress through Partnership*, p. 19.

52. See T. HAASE, K. McKEOWN, and S. ROURKE (1996), *Evaluation of the Global Grant, 1992-1995*, Kieran McKeown Ltd., Dublin (forthcoming).

53. See, for example, HARVEY, Brian (1994), *Combatting Exclusion. Lessons from the Third EU Poverty Programme in Ireland 1989-1994*, Combat Poverty Agency, Dublin.

54. The partnership is credited with having a very clearly defined "brokerage" approach to its work. The evaluation of the first twelve PESP partnerships identified distinctions in the operation of the partnerships between those that concentrated on service provision and those that had either an "agency" or "brokerage" role.

55. Plato Central Support Unit (1995), "A Feasibility Study on the Potential Development of Plato in Ireland", for the Department of Enterprise, p. 13.

56. Office of the Tanaiste (1995), *Interim Report of the Task Force on Long-Term Unemployment*, Government Publications, Dublin.

57. HARVEY, Brian (1994), *Combatting Exclusion*, pp. 32-33.

58. HANNAN and COMMINS, "The Significance of Small-scale Landowners in Ireland's Agricultural Transformation" in *The Development of Industrial Society*, J.H. GOLDTHORPE and C.T. WHELAN, eds., p. 81.

59. For a discussion of the current situation in rural Ireland and a thoughtful evaluation of the LEADER I programme, see KEARNEY, B., G. E. BOYLE and J.A. WALSH (1994), *EU LEADER I Initiative in Ireland. Evaluation and Recommendations*, Department of Agriculture, Food and Forestry, Dublin.

60. HANNAN and COMMINS, "The Significance of Small-scale Landowners", p. 84.

61. NESC (1995), *A New Approach to Rural Development*, Dublin.

62. For discussion of the skills needed to take advantage of the opportunities provided by the diversification of markets, see OECD (1995), *Niche Markets as a Rural Development Strategy*.

63. On this subject see NESC, *New Approaches to Rural Development*, pp. 148-9.

64. For current discussion of situated learning and related topics in the US see http://www.coled.umn.edu/iciwww/schooltowork/.

65. With its additional staffing, ADM has started to put in place some co-ordination mechanisms. For example, ADM, with Technical Assistance funding, is supporting a management development programme for partnership managers and training programmes for Board members from the social partner organisations and community groups. Moreover, a "Bureau" consisting of five representatives elected by the partnerships will now meet regularly with the Interdepartmental Policy Committee on Local Development and three times a year with the Minister for Local Development.

66. This situation may improve in the future because ICTU has put in place an extensive support structure for representatives on local partnerships, organised by ADM and funded through Technical Assistance.

Annex 1

A SPEECH BY TAOISEACH JOHN BRUTON

The consensus forged among the social partners and the government has elevated concern about long-term unemployment and related social problems and given further motivation to the community activism which drives the local development partnerships. In the opinion of the study group members, this broad political support was demonstrated by the Taoiseach Mr. John Bruton, T.D. in a speech:

I think we all know that in our own lives it's through bringing the best out in people, through co-operation that we actually achieve things; but when we enter politics or administration, we tend to forget that. In the way we administer programmes, we tend to think that people are like things. They're objects and you can move them around, when in fact they are people who are in poverty or people who have as many ideas and many more perhaps than we have ourselves. We need to approach a solution to their problems in such a way that it engages their creativity. That very simply is what the partnership approach is all about... We should focus on the needs of each individual unemployed person and seek to mobilise all the different resources that are available to tackle the problem of each individual individually, rather than simply applying mass solutions across the board... Obviously the idea of giving money to organisations to allow them to plan their own future, runs against one of the cardinal instincts of all of us who are involved in public administration, |which| is that things should be neat. Things should be simple... You've really got to accept that there are going to be people making mistakes... You've got to, to some degree at least, remove the control features in your thinking and apply a different approach |that allows| people to master their own destiny, to make their own mistakes and learn from them... You can't give power to somebody unless someone else gives it up. That's essentially it. Administrators have to be willing to give up some power so that those who are poor or who are in poverty and who need and want to develop can exercise some power.*

---

* Speech by Taoiseach Mr. John Bruton, T.D., at the opening of the EU Poverty 3 Programme, 25 April 1995.

Annex 2

DEVELOPMENT PARTNERSHIPS AND POLITICAL SYSTEMS

Contribution by Dr. Hans Pflaumer

LOCAL POLICY MAKING THROUGH PARTNERSHIPS?

There has hardly been a time when the public debate in OECD countries has concentrated as much as today on the necessity of innovation on almost all levels and in all sectors of society, notably in government. On the other hand, it appears that innovations are in especially short supply with the latter.

It is, therefore, anything but usual that the Irish Government, together with the social partners, was able to design and to realise a concept putting matters of great social and economic relevance like unemployment, poverty and exclusion in the centre of political consideration and activity. The Partnerships (ABPs) were founded on the initiative of the Government of Ireland (actually the Prime Minister) in co-operation with the social partners and then handed down and financed "from above" to the local level where, today, quite a number of them are working with obvious success.

Most member countries of the European Union are confronted with similar problems like, for instance, the irritating fact that – unlike in the past – positive economic growth rates have an increasingly weaker effect on the rate of unemployment, and that the number of long-term unemployed is constantly growing, provoking all the known consequences of impoverishment and social exclusion. While governments are struggling to find solutions to this dilemma and resulting social unrest (witness the strike wave in France at the end of 1995), traditional concepts still outnumber new and innovative ideas. All the more reason to seek examples where such innovations are emerging, especially those already in a phase of implementation or, at least, experimentation.

It is perhaps less surprising that in Ireland it was possible to arrive at an "all-party, all-sector consensus on the need for strong policies to address the issues of unemployment, poverty and exclusion" than that this consensus was indeed strong enough to allow for its implementation – which in the usual political set-up is the stumbling block for many a good idea. Very often, it is in the implementation phase when the actors become aware of what they might lose – and then don't go on to look for what they might win.

As it seems, this has not happened with the ABP concept in Ireland. Focusing on the aspects of ABPs and local government, the most striking innovative feature of the concept is what might be called the "grafting" of an additional level on to the local level. It may be argued that the partnerships are not intended to be political bodies such as local governments, and they indeed are not. On the other hand, it would be very difficult to maintain that they are non-political bodies in the broader sense of not designing policies and trying to implement them. This is their mandate, and this is precisely what they are doing.

As the study shows, this cannot be and, indeed is not, to everybody's delight. It is quite obvious that in order to fulfil their mandate, the partnerships have to deal with and influence local economic development, thereby, at least potentially, infringing on one of the core responsibilities of local government. And, indeed, the exclusion of local government representatives from the partnerships on first sight is a somewhat bizarre feature in the political-administrative structure of a "republican"-democratic country. It is not only the fact that these partnerships receive and spend public money without the traditional procedures and instruments of control by the democratically-elected representatives that evokes criticism. More surprisingly, by their activities – at least wherever they are successful – they seem to bring about a general change of political atmosphere and in this way insert an informal element of political youthfulness and competition into the political process of their communities.

Having had the privilege of visiting a number of partnerships and speaking with participants from these bodies as well as representatives of local governments, one gets the impression that this new approach may serve to escape from a self-inflicted, however common political impasse which might be described as "one-level problems and solutions": national problems are solved on the national level, local problems on the local level. Although this is a model of perfect simplicity and clarity, we have learned that it does not correspond to real life where problems frequently are multi-level, interlinked, and solutions must be found accordingly.

Governments must solve problems. Like everybody else, they prefer simple problems to more complicated ones. Problems demanding solutions across different government agencies are, for obvious reasons, more dreaded than others and sometimes are not solved for that very reason. The concept of the ABPs in Ireland is different in that it pulls together national resources across agency-dividing lines, at the same time transferring them to the local level and mandating the partnerships to seek locally adequate solutions for the national problem of long-term unemployment, poverty and exclusion. The study maintains that, to this day, a clear-cut description of the structure of the existing ABPs is not possible and that they can best be described by their projects. Yet there is one basic feature common at least to the partnerships visited by the study-group: the community spirit of those working in the partnerships, inspiring and enabling them to put to use their knowledge, their network of communications and influence for the benefit of those citizens in their community who are most in need of help and who in the past have not sufficiently been reached by national programmes.

If this core element of the partnerships can be sustained, other questions like the seeming duality between them and local government and, hence, the problem of democratic control and representation might be considered secondary: secondary not in their political significance, but in time. Sooner or later, the need to deal with this problem may become more urgent. It might be wise to think about this while the experimental phase of the partnership concept is still going strong and the political climate in Ireland is willing to accept the existence of some structural democratic "peculiarities" in exchange.

A SHORT GLANCE AT GERMANY

The phenomenon of long-term unemployment and the consequences on the social situation of the people concerned do exist in Germany, as they do in Ireland and in most European countries. The prospect for a substantial reduction of unemployment in the near future is dim, to say the least. The approach taken in Germany to this problem is different from Ireland for various reasons.

- Germany is a federal republic. Federalism here is not only a formal constitutional principle; it rather permeates the entire political process of the country in a substantial as well as procedural way. There is, of course, the perennial constitutional debate as to whether there exists in Germany three levels of government (federal, state and local) or just two (federal and state, whereby the communities are integrated parts of the federal states). But it is undisputed that the federal government must respect state jurisdiction when dealing with local governments. The federal government, for instance, cannot simply decide on financial support for urban renewal in cities and communities. It will have to enter into an agreement with all federal states on ways and volume of such support (Art. 104a IV of the German Constitution) and leave it to the discretion of state governments to distribute these finances according to the criteria set out in the agreement with the federal states.

- It follows that the federal government could not – as did the government of the Republic of Ireland – call into life anything comparable to ABPs on a local level, and that in order for anything like this to happen it would have to be negotiated with the federal states and not just with the social partners, thus multiplying the possibilities for political disagreement and slowing down the decision-making process. Moreover, the federal government is not a social partner (unless it acts in its capacity as employer of its civil servants) and, hence, does not have the relevant responsibilities as does the Government of Ireland (negotiating labour contracts, for example).

- It is interesting to note that in the last years of the 19th century in Germany the need for employment activities was seen on a local basis, and, especially in the larger cities, local employment services were established. In the face of growing unemployment after World War I, it was however felt that local employment services lacked the necessary overview of the labour market and that, therefore, a national institution was required with an overall responsibility for the German labour market. This institution was the predecessor of today's Federal Agency for Employment (*Bundesanstalt für Arbeit, BA*), an agency of public law with the right of self-administration. It is the federal agency responsible for practically all relevant matters of employment, unemployment insurance, further vocational training, etc., with a great number of sub-offices throughout the country. The right of self-administration is not only reflected in the structure of the head office but also throughout the entire system down to the sub-agency level with administrative committees composed of one-third employers' associations, labour/trade unions, and the public sector.

- Much as this seems to be a local element in the structure and procedure of the BA, for a long time debate had been going on about the desirability of an opening of these operations to possible activities of the private sector on a local level. The arguments used in favour of such an opening were frequently based on the experience that institutions of the size and the structure of the BA tend to be slow in recognising and responding to new situations and necessities, especially on a local level. Accordingly, legislation has been passed recently allowing private employment services to operate, provided they are licensed by a BA State Employment Agency.

- Under the Federal Subsistence Act, persons no longer eligible to receive unemployment benefits (mainly because of long-term unemployment) and other persons with an income below the subsistence level are entitled to receive subsistence money from their local government. To these governments, the increasing number of persons eligible for this kind of support represents a heavy financial burden. Many local authorities have in the meanwhile started to offer jobs with limited contracts to persons eligible to subsistence benefits with the intention to prepare them to return to the normal labour market after a long period of unemployment.

From this short survey, it may be clear that the structure of the German "social security net", while being strong and densely knit, differs considerably from the Irish approach. On the other hand, the study has shown that some of the basic problems in this field are very similar.

What is so intriguing in the Irish approach is the attempt, in many partnerships, to combine employment with entrepreneurship, the creation of new jobs for people looking for them in the same community. Focusing on this aspect one might say that, while a great number of new jobs have been created and are being created in Germany, the local combination of supporting qualification, job creation and employment is an objective worth following up further in Germany. There is, however, one very specific important factor in the Irish approach: the community spirit. Granted that this, among other things, has definitive historical roots in the Great Famine (18), it would seem a bit fatalistic to accept that a strong community spirit has little chance to be developed in other countries with comparable needs and requirements as in Ireland.

As far as Germany is concerned, the seeming institutional barriers – as indicated above – to a new or additional approach need not be insurmountable. The existing institutions will, however, have to be integrated in any new concept. It would be hard to imagine any workable solution on a local level which would not include local government – as is the case in Ireland. The entrepreneurial element would have to be injected into the scheme, and for this to happen an active community spirit might be the right carrier.

As in any traditional political system, changes do not come about by themselves, and if they do at all they come about slowly. The time for a new approach in Germany may, however, be favourable. The Federal Government has just decided a "Programme for Investments and Employment" (*Aktionsprogramm für Investitionen und Arbeitsplätze*) which seeks to reduce the present level of unemployment by half by the year 2000. Industry and the labour unions have started negotiations on a "Pact for Work and Employment", which seeks to reduce the present level of unemployment by half by the year 2000. Further, industry and the labour unions have started negotiations on a "Pact for Work and Employment", aimed at the creation of new jobs.

These are important initiatives, and, while the ways and means currently under discussion seem to be rather more conventional than innovative, there may be a chance for a new approach based on the full use of community spirit and local contributions to the solution of this task. Models and experiments perhaps are the best way to get started.

Annex 3

LOCAL DEVELOPMENT IN FINLAND AND IRELAND

Contribution by Paavo Saikkonen

There are many obvious similarities between Ireland and Finland. Both are relatively small countries on the periphery of continental Europe and, in comparison to other European countries, both are young nations, having been involved in prolonged struggles for independence. In terms of economic policy, both are now very open economies and sensitive to international fluctuations. The two countries are also similar in facing severe unemployment problems, though the problem developed differently in each case. Ireland experienced increasing rates of unemployment from 1980 onwards, with a modest recovery in 1987 followed by another surge after 1990. The peculiar aspect of the Irish situation was that worsening unemployment rates were accompanied by rates of economic growth which compared favourably with all other OECD countries. In Finland, employment levels were high throughout the 1980s, even approaching full employment, and the appearance of high levels of unemployment came suddenly and without warning. The causes of this deep recession, from which Finland is only now starting to recover, included a slump in the world market for pulp and paper products, one of Finland's two main exports (the other being metallurgy and engineering), the collapse of the Soviet market in 1989-90 and banking crises sparked by the Central Bank's deregulation of the currency markets in the second half of the 1980s. The speed and severity of this transition has affected every aspect of life in Finland and put government policies, particularly those dealing with social welfare, under enormous pressure.

In this sense, Ireland has a particular advantage in coping with the impacts of unemployment. Faced with a gradually deteriorating employment situation, the Irish government has implemented and evaluated a huge range of different policy responses, learning many important lessons in the process. In Finland, mass unemployment is a new phenomenon and the government has little in the way of personal experience on which to draw. Long-term unemployment in particular is a completely new experience. The initial response of the Finnish Ministry of Labour was to continue to fly the flag of full employment and promote active labour market policies in true Scandinavian style. However, an increasingly large share of labour market expenditure was, and is, being soaked up by passive benefit payments to the unemployed, limiting the effective ability of the Finnish authorities to prioritise active labour market policies in the short term or experiment with local projects.

On the other hand, local development as a policy approach is well-known in Finland and for a number of reasons local development groups have advantages not shared by their counterparts in Ireland. First, municipal governments have historically been very autonomous, with extensive taxation rights. Despite a lack of scale and limited resources, the municipalities have wide experience of organising their own development projects. Another asset is the decentralised university system: local universities participate actively in local development initiatives and in many instances have been the main mobilising agent.

The evolution of the system of public administration has also encouraged local development. Finland has, in recent years, relied on the three Ds principle – delegation, decentralisation and deregulation. Take, for example, the Labour Market Service. At the beginning of the 1990s, the management by results system was introduced which gave much greater decision making freedom to the 13 Finnish labour market districts and 200 employment offices. In all areas of policy design and implementation, the autonomy of district and local officials has increased dramatically in the past few years. The role of the Ministry of Labour has likewise developed towards a consolidated management strategy through which the district administrations are directed using strategic outlines, funding granted for the implementation of these strategic plan and then monitoring the implementation of the plans.

The central importance of local initiatives in the overall strategy of the Ministry of Labour is shown by the Structural Change Scheme, introduced towards the end of the 1980s, which emphasises such projects as creating networks among local firms and between public and private actors. The role of the central government has been to facilitate the development of these networks and act as a catalyst for the development of projects. The essence of the approach is that projects should be based on practical problems, adapted to local circumstances, and implemented quickly in response to local needs.

The lessons from this experience with local initiatives have to some extent been carried into the new fight against unemployment. For example, within the past eighteen months, the government has launched two major employment creation initiatives that stress local development approaches. In 1994, the new President of Finland inaugurated a Presidential Working Group on Employment which took as its objective the reduction of unemployment from half a million to 200 000 by the end of the decade. Among the various macroeconomics measures foreseen in the report of the Working Group, there were two proposals for the introduction of local employment creation initiatives and the development of cooperatives for the unemployed. A subsequent government "Programme for the Halving of Unemployment in

Finland" set out five specific proposals to encourage local efforts at employment creation.

Yet, despite the favourable institutional arrangement and the recent impulses provided by the central government in consultation with local authorities, local development appears to be much more active and imaginative in Ireland than in Finland. As is discussed in the description of the Area-Based Partnerships, the initiative was introduced by departments of the central administration. The manner in which these programmes were introduced is obviously unusual, yet it does not explain why the initiatives appear to be so vigorous and effective in comparison to locally-driven and designed programmes run by central and local governments in Finland.

A variety of economic, political and sociocultural explanations of this paradox could be proposed. Firstly, one could argue that the arrival of unemployment was initially viewed as a temporary problem caused by adverse economic fluctuations in Finland's main export sectors. The response of the government was to try to revive flagging exports and in so doing reverse the economic trends that were generating unemployment. Indeed, the policy adopted by the government between 1991 and 1995, in particular its monetary policy, was successful in rejuvenating export industries. Two devaluations of the national currency plus industrial restructuring recreated Finland's competitive edge in the production of pulp and paper and the sector enjoyed a mini-boom in 1995. However, in terms of employment creation the policy was a catastrophe. The restructuring of extractive and manufacturing industries in Finland over the course of five years had profoundly changed labour demand, and in the meantime, the government had done little adjust labour supply. The underlying causes of unemployment in Finland were not addressed during the period largely because there was a general assumption that macroeconomics and industrial policy adjustments would work as they had done in the past. The symptoms, however, had changed and the old medicine no longer brought relief. At the same time the conviction that the traditional remedies needed time to take effect inhibited the development of alternative policy approaches – as a result, economic and social adversity did not bring local action to the forefront of policy making as it did in Ireland.

Another reason that Finnish local development efforts seem constrained is that people depend on the state to establish and direct development work. The private sector, which as we have seen plays a crucial role in the success of many Area-Based Partnership activities, is uninvolved in Finland. Public-private partnerships are still rare. In Ireland, the importance of including private enterprises and NGOs in local development groups is widely accepted. This is not the case in Finland, with the result that local development activities are usually governmental in nature and follow the general formulas of bureaucratic programme design. This reliance on the public sector to take the lead is currently changing but only slowly.

The Area-Based Partnerships and other local development partnership groups have a number of important lessons that Finland could learn from.

- The partnership companies bring together the long-term unemployed, employers, statutory agencies and voluntary/community groups at the local level for concrete activities. in Finland, the tripartite bargaining structure is important in terms of creating consensual policy at the national, but has not been involved in implementing policy on the ground. Voluntary groups likewise play only a modest role in policy action in Finland. The partnerships in Ireland permit a range of local actors to pool resources and address local problems in a way that the central government agencies cannot. In Finland, there is still too much reliance on the central government to design and manage all aspects of employment creation and economic development.

- The role of the partnerships is to complement the activities of government agencies not to compete with them. The existence of one does not deny the legitimacy of the other. In Finland, the Ministry of Labour is overwhelmed by the challenge of 400 000 new job-seekers. It does not have the time to set up Speedpaks or Paksorts. In each administrative system there must be those who have the breathing space to experiment. At present, this kind of institution is lacking in Finland.

- The ability of the Partnerships to experiment and try new policy approaches has been aided by their legal company status. This enables them to circumvent much of the usual red tape and many of the responsibilities accruing to a normal central or local governmental agency that restrict freedom of manœuvre.

- The use of seconded staff from statutory agencies serves to maintain a link between the Partnerships and the central government. The issue of legitimacy, which would be important in the Finnish context, is somewhat reduced by the system of having a limited permanent staff (usually a manager and a secretary) in each local development group and then seconding expert personnel from FÁS, VEC or the Centres for the Unemployed.

- The position of ADM as an independent co-ordinating body appears to be an important innovation. The system as a whole is made more flexible by the fact that there is a private management company in between the partnerships and the central government. By virtue of its limited company status, ADM is able to act as an intermediary body rather than simply a control instrument of the central government. This sense of impartiality is reinforced by the fact that ADM's Board is composed of representatives of the social partners as well as of central government.

- Finally, there is tendency in Finland, as elsewhere, to think that if one activity overlaps with another then this represents duplication and the programmes must be "rationalised". However, the Irish example, where local development groups are tackling multifaceted problems of unemployment and social exclusion, suggests that sometimes situations are too complex to be put under one roof – the tendency of groups to address unemployment by looking at the local environment or housing situation will always raise questions of overlap with other agencies. But this seems to be almost inevitable and perhaps must be accepted in order to arrive at the synergies that animate local development in Ireland.

CONCLUSION

All this is not to say that local development in Ireland is perfect and in Finland a disaster. On the contrary, Finland is, in general, very receptive to the notion of local development and can be proud of a number of projects that have been introduced in recent years. Nevertheless, the Irish appear to have been superior to most countries in their emphasis on the area-based approach to combating economic and social problems. Despite the fact that the programmes are of a limited scale and can only contribute in a small way to reducing unemployment, they effectively target the most disadvantaged groups and, through the particular partnership approach used, they involve local people in the project of their own regeneration. The extent to which local people have been allowed to design the local development strategy is suggested by the wide disparity in priorities and methods among the various partnership groups.

One of the main strengths of the Partnership programme is its experimental nature. nobody could predict in advance how the groups would take on the challenge presented to them by the Department of the Taoiseach. However, there was an implicit confidence in the capability and imagination of local people. The Finnish approach has until now concentrated much more on planning-led, programme-based strategies directed through government agencies, but the Irish example proves that local actors can be effective, responsible partners for central government. A vital lesson to learn from the Irish experience is that a programme seasoned with a few drops of experimentalism can generate creative and productive results.

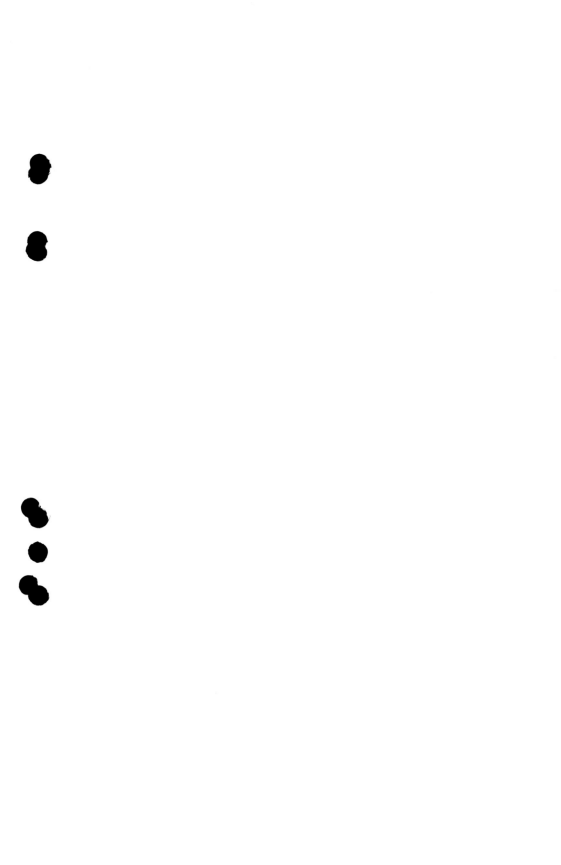

MAIN SALES OUTLETS OF OECD PUBLICATIONS
PRINCIPAUX POINTS DE VENTE DES PUBLICATIONS DE L'OCDE

ARGENTINA – ARGENTINE
Carlos Hirsch S.R.L.
Galería Güemes, Florida 165, 4° Piso
1333 Buenos Aires   Tel. (1) 331.1787 y 331.2391
                           Telefax: (1) 331.1787

AUSTRALIA – AUSTRALIE
D.A. Information Services
648 Whitehorse Road, P.O.B 163
Mitcham, Victoria 3132   Tel. (03) 9210.7777
                           Telefax: (03) 9210.7788

AUSTRIA – AUTRICHE
Gerold & Co.
Graben 31
Wien I   Tel. (0222) 533.50.14
                           Telefax: (0222) 512.47.31.29

BELGIUM – BELGIQUE
Jean De Lannoy
Avenue du Roi 202 Koningslaan
B-1060 Bruxelles   Tel. (02) 538.51.69/538.08.41
                           Telefax: (02) 538.08.41

CANADA
Renouf Publishing Company Ltd.
1294 Algoma Road
Ottawa, ON K1B 3W8   Tel. (613) 741.4333
                           Telefax: (613) 741.5439
Stores:
61 Sparks Street
Ottawa, ON K1P 5R1   Tel. (613) 238.8985
12 Adelaide Street West
Toronto, ON M5H 1L6   Tel. (416) 363.3171
                           Telefax: (416)363.59.63

Les Éditions La Liberté Inc.
3020 Chemin Sainte-Foy
Sainte-Foy, PQ G1X 3V6   Tel. (418) 658.3763
                           Telefax: (418) 658.3763

Federal Publications Inc.
165 University Avenue, Suite 701
Toronto, ON M5H 3B8   Tel. (416) 860.1611
                           Telefax: (416) 860.1608

Les Publications Fédérales
1185 Université
Montréal, QC H3B 3A7   Tel. (514) 954.1633
                           Telefax: (514) 954.1635

CHINA – CHINE
China National Publications Import
Export Corporation (CNPIEC)
16 Gongti E. Road, Chaoyang District
P.O. Box 88 or 50
Beijing 100704 PR   Tel. (01) 506.6688
                           Telefax: (01) 506.3101

CHINESE TAIPEI – TAIPEI CHINOIS
Good Faith Worldwide Int'l. Co. Ltd.
9th Floor, No. 118, Sec. 2
Chung Hsiao E. Road
Taipei   Tel. (02) 391.7396/391.7397
                           Telefax: (02) 394.9176

**CZECH REPUBLIC –
RÉPUBLIQUE TCHÈQUE**
Artia Pegas Press Ltd.
Narodni Trida 25
POB 825
111 21 Praha 1   Tel. (2) 242 246 04
                           Telefax: (2) 242 278 72

DENMARK – DANEMARK
Munksgaard Book and Subscription Service
35, Nørre Søgade, P.O. Box 2148
DK-1016 København K   Tel. (33) 12.85.70
                           Telefax: (33) 12.93.87

EGYPT – ÉGYPTE
Middle East Observer
41 Sherif Street
Cairo   Tel. 392.6919
                           Telefax: 360-6804

FINLAND – FINLANDE
Akateeminen Kirjakauppa
Keskuskatu 1, P.O. Box 128
00100 Helsinki

Subscription Services/Agence d'abonnements :
P.O. Box 23
00371 Helsinki   Tel. (358 0) 121 4416
                           Telefax: (358 0) 121.4450

FRANCE
OECD/OCDE
Mail Orders/Commandes par correspondance :
2, rue André-Pascal
75775 Paris Cedex 16   Tel. (33-1) 45.24.82.00
                           Telefax: (33-1) 49.10.42.76
                           Telex: 640048 OCDE
Internet: Compte.PUBSINQ @ oecd.org
Orders via Minitel, France only/
Commandes par Minitel, France exclusivement :
36 15 OCDE
OECD Bookshop/Librairie de l'OCDE :
33, rue Octave-Feuillet
75016 Paris   Tel. (33-1) 45.24.81.81
                           (33-1) 45.24.81.67
Dawson
B.P. 40
91121 Palaiseau Cedex   Tel. 69.10.47.00
                           Telefax : 64.54.83.26

Documentation Française
29, quai Voltaire
75007 Paris   Tel. 40.15.70.00

Economica
49, rue Héricart
75015 Paris   Tel. 45.78.12.92
                           Telefax : 40.58.15.70

Gibert Jeune (Droit-Économie)
6, place Saint-Michel
75006 Paris   Tel. 43.25.91.19

Librairie du Commerce International
10, avenue d'Iéna
75016 Paris   Tel. 40.73.34.60

Librairie Dunod
Université Paris-Dauphine
Place du Maréchal-de-Lattre-de-Tassigny
75016 Paris   Tel. 44.05.40.13

Librairie Lavoisier
11, rue Lavoisier
75008 Paris   Tel. 42.65.39.95

Librairie des Sciences Politiques
30, rue Saint-Guillaume
75007 Paris   Tel. 45.48.36.02

P.U.F.
49, boulevard Saint-Michel
75005 Paris   Tel. 43.25.83.40

Librairie de l'Université
12a, rue Nazareth
13100 Aix-en-Provence   Tel. (16) 42.26.18.08

Documentation Française
165, rue Garibaldi
69003 Lyon   Tel. (16) 78.63.32.23

Librairie Decitre
29, place Bellecour
69002 Lyon   Tel. (16) 72.40.54.54

Librairie Sauramps
Le Triangle
34967 Montpellier Cedex 2 Tel. (16) 67.58.85.15
                           Tekefax: (16) 67.58.27.36

A la Sorbonne Actual
23, rue de l'Hôtel-des-Postes
06000 Nice   Tel. (16) 93.13.77.75
                           Telefax: (16) 93.80.75.69

GERMANY – ALLEMAGNE
OECD Publications and Information Centre
August-Bebel-Allee 6
D-53175 Bonn   Tel. (0228) 959.120
                           Telefax: (0228) 959.12.17

GREECE – GRÈCE
Librairie Kauffmann
Mavrokordatou 9
106 78 Athens   Tel. (01) 32.55.321
                           Telefax: (01) 32.30.320

HONG-KONG
Swindon Book Co. Ltd.
Astoria Bldg. 3F
34 Ashley Road, Tsimshatsui
Kowloon, Hong Kong   Tel. 2376.2062
                           Telefax: 2376.0685

HUNGARY – HONGRIE
Euro Info Service
Margitsziget, Európa Ház
1138 Budapest   Tel. (1) 111.62.16
                           Telefax: (1) 111.60.61

ICELAND – ISLANDE
Mál Mog Menning
Laugavegi 18, Pósthólf 392
121 Reykjavik   Tel. (1) 552.4240
                           Telefax: (1) 562.3523

INDIA – INDE
Oxford Book and Stationery Co.
Scindia House
New Delhi 110001   Tel. (11) 331.5896/5308
                           Telefax: (11) 332.5993
17 Park Street
Calcutta 700016   Tel. 240832

INDONESIA – INDONÉSIE
Pdii-Lipi
P.O. Box 4298
Jakarta 12042   Tel. (21) 573.34.67
                           Telefax: (21) 573.34.67

IRELAND – IRLANDE
Government Supplies Agency
Publications Section
4/5 Harcourt Road
Dublin 2   Tel. 661.31.11
                           Telefax: 475.27.60

ISRAEL – ISRAËL
Praedicta
5 Shatner Street
P.O. Box 34030
Jerusalem 91430   Tel. (2) 52.84.90/1/2
                           Telefax: (2) 52.84.93

R.O.Y. International
P.O. Box 13056
Tel Aviv 61130   Tel. (3) 546 1423
                           Telefax: (3) 546 1442

Palestinian Authority/Middle East:
INDEX Information Services
P.O.B. 19502
Jerusalem   Tel. (2) 27.12.19
                           Telefax: (2) 27.16.34

ITALY – ITALIE
Libreria Commissionaria Sansoni
Via Duca di Calabria 1/1
50125 Firenze   Tel. (055) 64.54.15
                           Telefax: (055) 64.12.57
Via Bartolini 29
20155 Milano   Tel. (02) 36.50.83

Editrice e Libreria Herder
Piazza Montecitorio 120
00186 Roma   Tel. 679.46.28
                                    Telefax: 678.47.51

Libreria Hoepli
Via Hoepli 5
20121 Milano   Tel. (02) 86.54.46
                                    Telefax: (02) 805.28.86

Libreria Scientifica
Dott. Lucio de Biasio 'Aeiou'
Via Coronelli, 6
20146 Milano   Tel. (02) 48.95.45.52
                                    Telefax: (02) 48.95.45.48

JAPAN – JAPON
OECD Publications and Information Centre
Landic Akasaka Building
2-3-4 Akasaka, Minato-ku
Tokyo 107   Tel. (81.3) 3586.2016
                                    Telefax: (81.3) 3584.7929

KOREA – CORÉE
Kyobo Book Centre Co. Ltd.
P.O. Box 1658, Kwang Hwa Moon
Seoul   Tel. 730.78.91
                                    Telefax: 735.00.30

MALAYSIA – MALAISIE
University of Malaya Bookshop
University of Malaya
P.O. Box 1127, Jalan Pantai Baru
59700 Kuala Lumpur
Malaysia   Tel. 756.5000/756.5425
                                    Telefax: 756.3246

MEXICO – MEXIQUE
OECD Publications and Information Centre
Edificio INFOTEC
Av. San Fernando no. 37
Col. Toriello Guerra
Tlalpan C.P. 14050
Mexico D.F.
                Tel. (525) 606 00 11 Extension 100
                Fax : (525) 606 13 07

Revistas y Periodicos Internacionales S.A. de C.V.
Florencia 57 - 1004
Mexico. D.F. 06600   Tel. 207.81.00
                                    Telefax: 208.39.79

NETHERLANDS – PAYS-BAS
SDU Uitgeverij Plantijnstraat
Externe Fondsen
Postbus 20014
2500 EA's-Gravenhage   Tel. (070) 37.89.880
Voor bestellingen: Telefax: (070) 34.75.778

NEW ZEALAND – NOUVELLE-ZÉLANDE
GPLegislation Services
P.O. Box 12418
Thorndon, Wellington   Tel. (04) 496.5655
                                    Telefax: (04) 496.5698

NORWAY – NORVÈGE
NIC INFO A/S
Bertrand Narvesens vei 2
P.O. Box 6512 Etterstad
0606 Oslo 6   Tel. (022) 57.33.00
                                    Telefax: (022) 68.19.01

PAKISTAN
Mirza Book Agency
65 Shahrah Quaid-E-Azam
Lahore 54000   Tel. (42) 353.601
                                    Telefax: (42) 231.730

PHILIPPINE – PHILIPPINES
International Booksource Center Inc.
Rm 179/920 Cityland 10 Condo Tower 2
HV dela Costa Ext cor Valero St.
Makati Metro Manila   Tel. (632) 817 9676
                                Telefax : (632) 817 1741

POLAND – POLOGNE
Ars Polona
00-950 Warszawa
Krakowskie Przedmieácie 7   Tel. (22) 264760
                                    Telefax : (22) 268673

PORTUGAL
Livraria Portugal
Rua do Carmo 70-74
Apart. 2681
1200 Lisboa   Tel. (01) 347.49.82/5
                                    Telefax: (01) 347.02.64

SINGAPORE – SINGAPOUR
Gower Asia Pacific Pte Ltd.
Golden Wheel Building
41, Kallang Pudding Road, No. 04-03
Singapore 1334   Tel. 741.5166
                                    Telefax: 742.9356

SPAIN – ESPAGNE
Mundi-Prensa Libros S.A.
Castelló 37, Apartado 1223
Madrid 28001   Tel. (91) 431.33.99
                                    Telefax: (91) 575.39.98

Mundi-Prensa Barcelona
Consell de Cent No. 391
08009 – Barcelona   Tel. (93) 488.34.92
                                    Telefax: (93) 487.76.59

Llibreria de la Generalitat
Palau Moja
Rambla dels Estudis, 118
08002 – Barcelona
                  (Subscripcions) Tel. (93) 318.80.12
                  (Publicacions) Tel. (93) 302.67.23
                                  Telefax: (93) 412.18.54

SRI LANKA
Centre for Policy Research
c/o Colombo Agencies Ltd.
No. 300-304, Galle Road
Colombo 3   Tel. (1) 574240, 573551-2
                             Telefax: (1) 575394, 510711

SWEDEN – SUÈDE
CE Fritzes AB
S–106 47 Stockholm   Tel. (08) 690.90.90
                                    Telefax: (08) 20.50.21

Subscription Agency/Agence d'abonnements :
Wennergren-Williams Info AB
P.O. Box 1305
171 25 Solna   Tel. (08) 705.97.50
                                    Telefax: (08) 27.00.71

SWITZERLAND – SUISSE
Maditec S.A. (Books and Periodicals - Livres
et périodiques)
Chemin des Palettes 4
Case postale 266
1020 Renens VD 1   Tel. (021) 635.08.65
                                    Telefax: (021) 635.07.80

Librairie Payot S.A.
4, place Pépinet
CP 3212
1002 Lausanne   Tel. (021) 320.25.11
                                    Telefax: (021) 320.25.14

Librairie Unilivres
6, rue de Candolle
1205 Genève   Tel. (022) 320.26.23
                                    Telefax: (022) 329.73.18

Subscription Agency/Agence d'abonnements :
Dynapresse Marketing S.A.
38 avenue Vibert
1227 Carouge   Tel. (022) 308.07.89
                                    Telefax: (022) 308.07.99

See also – Voir aussi :
OECD Publications and Information Centre
August-Bebel-Allee 6
D-53175 Bonn (Germany)   Tel. (0228) 959.120
                                    Telefax: (0228) 959.12.17

THAILAND – THAÏLANDE
Suksit Siam Co. Ltd.
113, 115 Fuang Nakhon Rd.
Opp. Wat Rajbopith
Bangkok 10200   Tel. (662) 225.9531/2
                                    Telefax: (662) 222.5188

TUNISIA – TUNISIE
Grande Librairie Spécialisée
Fendri Ali
Avenue Haffouz Imm El-Intilaka
Bloc B 1 Sfax 3000   Tel. (216-4) 296 855
                                    Telefax: (216-4) 298.270

TURKEY – TURQUIE
Kültür Yayinlari Is-Türk Ltd. Sti.
Atatürk Bulvari No. 191/Kat 13
Kavaklidere/Ankara
                        Tel. (312) 428.11.40 Ext. 2458
                             Telefax: (312) 417 24 90
Dolmabahce Cad. No. 29
Besiktas/Istanbul   Tel. (212) 260 7188

UNITED KINGDOM – ROYAUME-UNI
HMSO
Gen. enquiries   Tel. (171) 873 8242
Postal orders only:
P.O. Box 276, London SW8 5DT
Personal Callers HMSO Bookshop
49 High Holborn, London WC1V 6HB
                                    Telefax: (171) 873 8416
Branches at: Belfast, Birmingham, Bristol,
Edinburgh, Manchester

UNITED STATES – ÉTATS-UNIS
OECD Publications and Information Center
2001 L Street N.W., Suite 650
Washington, D.C. 20036-4922   Tel. (202) 785.6323
                                    Telefax: (202) 785.0350

Subscriptions to OECD periodicals may also be placed
through main subscription agencies.

Les abonnements aux publications périodiques de
l'OCDE peuvent être souscrits auprès des principales
agences d'abonnement.

Orders and inquiries from countries where Distributors
have not yet been appointed should be sent to: OECD
Publications Service, 2, rue André-Pascal, 75775 Paris
Cedex 16, France.

Les commandes provenant de pays où l'OCDE n'a pas
encore désigné de distributeur peuvent être adressées à :
OCDE, Service des Publications, 2, rue André-Pascal,
75775 Paris Cedex 16, France.

                                            1-1996

OECD PUBLICATIONS, 2, rue André-Pascal, 75775 PARIS CEDEX 16
PRINTED IN FRANCE
(04 96 05 1) ISBN 92-64-14878-7 – No. 48665 1996

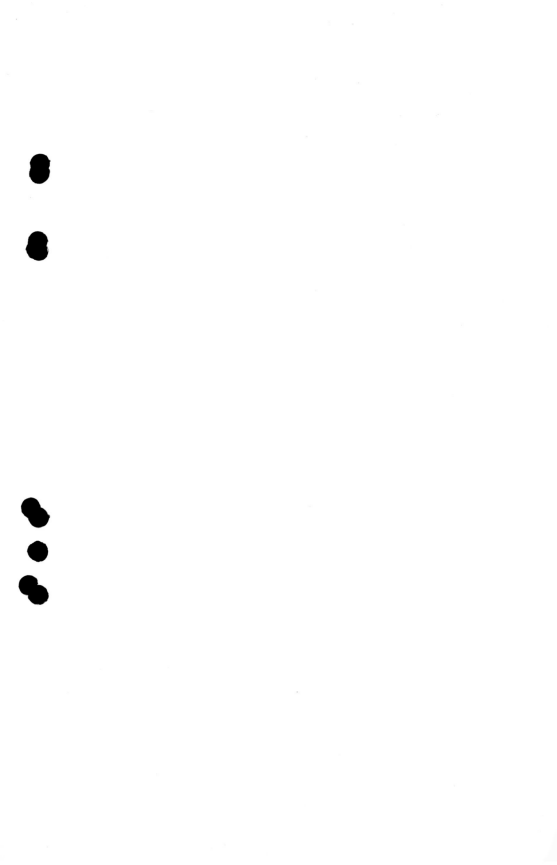